THE CHANGING FACE OF LIVERPOOL
1207 - 1770

 Merseyside Archaeological Society 2007

Figure 1: *Yates and Perry map of the Environs of Liverpool dated 1768.*

Acknowledgements

This project received generous financial support from the Liverpool Culture Company Ltd. and Liverpool City Council as part of the In The City Grants Programme 06-07. Additional expenditure has been met by a donation from a long-standing member of Merseyside Archaeological Society who wishes to remain anonymous.

The project team comprises the following:

Barry Faulkner, Roy Fletcher, Kay Fox, David Harthen, Len Kata, Peter Lucas, Julia McLaughlin Cook, Dorothy O'Hanlon, Dave Roberts and Pauline Roberts.

Editors: Julia McLaughlin Cook and Dave Roberts.
Layout and Artwork: Dave Roberts.

Particular thanks are due to Julia McLaughlin Cook who led most of the research activities and David Harthen who gave academic guidance. Additional thanks are due to Jenny Woodcock and Roy Forshaw for their assistance.

We would like to thank the staff of the following institutions:
Merseyside Archaeological Service for giving access to and help with interpreting the contents of the Merseyside Sites and Monuments Record and for providing photographs.
Liverpool Record Office, Liverpool Central Libraries (particularly Roger Hull for assistance with providing the illustrations).
National Museums Liverpool, Field Archaeology Unit for their support and for providing photographs of their work.

We owe a debt of gratitude to the team that produced "The Changing Face of Liverpool 1207-1727" in 1982, whose work was invaluable in the production of this book.

We would like to thank all our friends and fellow members of Merseyside Archaeological Society for their suggestions, encouragement and tireless support in this endeavour.

Dave Roberts
Secretary, Merseyside Archaeological Society
March 2007

ISBN 0 906479 04 5

CONTENTS

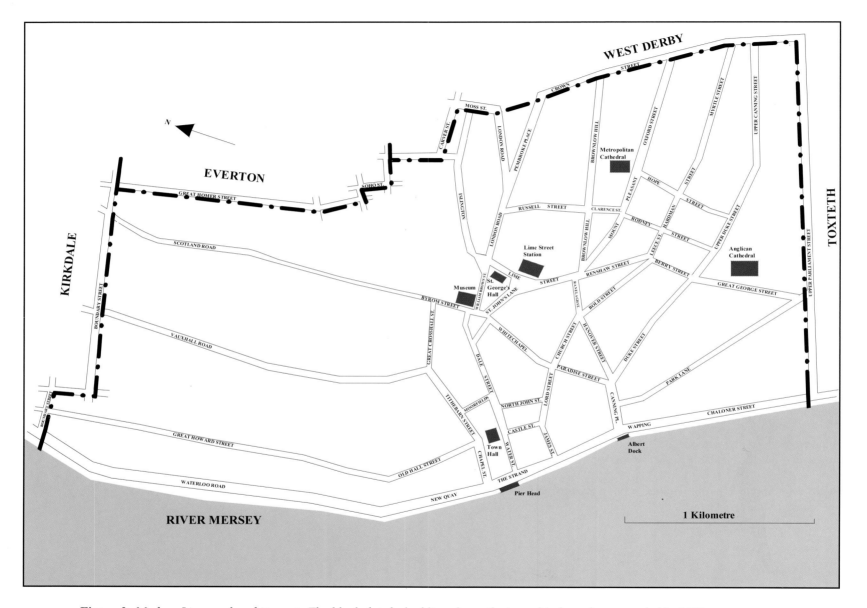

Figure 2: *Modern Liverpool and its past. The black dot-dashed line shows the township boundary recorded in 1671 as interpreted by James Touzeau (Touzeau 1910, 283).*

Introduction

This book is about the medieval town of Liverpool and the area of the post-medieval township, which remained a separate administrative unit until the boundary changes of 1835. Liverpool was bounded by Kirkdale, Everton and West Derby townships and Toxteth Park. Today this area forms the heart of the city of Liverpool and its separate identity is hard to imagine. The growth of the town in the period from 1207 to 1770 is traced through its principal sites and buildings as they have been revealed through documentary research and archaeological activity.

The records paint a picture of a small coastal borough, typical of the limited scope of English urban life remote from the capital before the spread of roads and railways. Throughout the first few centuries the main occupations were agriculture and sea-borne trade. The population fluctuated in size, but grew very little until the second half of the seventeenth century. After the upheavals of the Civil War, the town expanded 'over the Pool'. The great increase in trade and the rise of industry changed the size and aspect of the town almost out of recognition.

The research for the first three periods covered by this project was undertaken between 1979 and 1981 and was published in 1982 as "The Changing Face of Liverpool". A whole generation of urban development has taken place since then so it was decided the time had come to update and expand the original work. "The Changing Face" chose as its closing image the 1728 Prospect of Liverpool engraved by Samuel and Nathanael Buck, which shows the river front of the town from across the Mersey. Behind a narrow ribbon of waterfront settlement are fields and windmills. We have chosen to end our survey with George Perry's 1769 "Plan of the Town and Port of Liverpool", which reveals the rapid expansion of the town in the intervening fifty years. This point in time covers the steady growth of the town in the early years of the Industrial Revolution. In 1774 the Leeds-Liverpool canal came to the town ushering in a period of even more rapid expansion which belongs to another story.

Sources

Since the first edition of this book appeared most archaeological work that has been carried out in the city has been funded by developers. Much of the archaeology revealed has related to Liverpool in the nineteenth and twentieth centuries, but some sites from before 1770 have been revealed. Between 2001 and 2006 work has been ongoing at Chavasse Park (the site of the Pool of Liverpool, which became the First Dock). Work was undertaken near the entrance to the Canning and Salthouse Docks as part of the Mersey Tram Project, and at Mann Island as part of the Canal Link. Little of this work has been published yet so only a few findings can be mentioned.

The only visible remnant of the medieval borough, apart from most of the H-shaped pattern of the original streets, is the 'sanctuary stone' in Castle Street. The oldest building

in the city centre is Bluecoat Chambers, which was begun in 1716 and lies outside the area of the first settlement. Therefore, most of what we know about the history of the town comes from old documents in published or calendar form. The main sources for the earliest period are the deeds of three families who played a large part in the early affairs of the town: the Crosse family, the Moores and the Norrises. From the sixteenth century onwards there are the Town Books and for the seventeenth century Parish Registers of St Nicholas's Church and the Moore Rental of 1668. For the eighteenth century there are Rate Assessment Books, Dock Records, the Diary of Nicholas Blundell, commercial documents, and Gore's Directory.

The first contemporary view of Liverpool is a 1680 painting now in the possession of National Museums Liverpool. The earliest known contemporary map is by James Chadwick in 1725. Sketches and paintings of earlier buildings and streets have to be assessed individually for accuracy as they were often merely copies or imaginative reconstructions. In the nineteenth century, the Herdman family of painters produced a number of views of an older Liverpool, some of which were based on earlier drawings or paintings, and some were their own imaginative reconstructions. The sketch maps in this book are compilations.

Figure 3: *View of Liverpool from the river 1680.*

How to Use the Book

At the beginning of the book there are a number of short sections which give an overview of various aspects of Liverpool's development from earliest times to the beginning of the nineteenth century. Each has been writtten by a different researcher hence the slight variation in style. For those who are interested in knowing more about a particular topic, there are numbers in brackets in the text, which correspond to notes at the back, for example note 1 in the Topography section refers the reader to Stewart-Brown 1932; this is a book written by Stewart-Brown in 1932 and the full title of this book is in the list of books at the back (bibliography). The bibliography is a list of the books and documents that have been consulted. There are lists at the back of maps and plans consulted and for the sources of the illustrations.

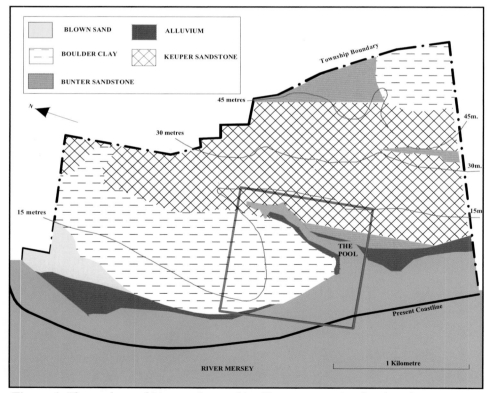

Figure 4: *The geology of Liverpool township. The square outined is that shown in figures 21, 24 and 29.*

Topography

Until the late seventeenth century, the town of Liverpool was confined to a sandstone peninsula overlooking the Wirral at one of the narrowest points of the Mersey estuary. It was separated from land to the south by the Pool, a stream that flowed into the Mersey, until the early 1700s when this was filled in. It is hard to see the town's original shape on the earliest map, Chadwick's map of 1725, as it shows the street plan superimposed on the recently reclaimed land. However, by combining evidence from contour and geological surveys with contemporary descriptions, it is possible to deduce the location and former extent of the Pool (1) and its feeder streams, and to get a picture of the soils and some of the natural vegetation before urban development (2).

The surface geology and ground contour were both formed in the Ice Age by the action of glaciers which left mineral debris scattered across the underlying, crudely abraded rock surface. Some sandstone was left exposed on the rising ground to the east of the Pool and in the area of the Castle mound west of the Pool. Quarrying is known to have taken place from as early as the sixteenth century onwards (3).

A peat bog, known as Moss Lake, existed on the table-land in the Abercromby Square/Falkner Square area (4). Not only was it a much-valued source of peat for fuel, but also it was the source of a stream which helped to power two Liverpool water mills. Pollen samples have been taken from the Moss Lake area but as they are from late-Glacial deposits they predate any known human activity in the vicinity (5).

West of the Pool, in the area of the medieval town, boulder clay covered most of the rock, though the castle itself was built directly on the sandstone (6). Wells in the sandstone under the town provided for some of the population's needs, and are mentioned in the 1540-1 Bylaws (7). The slopes on either side of the main ridge line of the present Old Hall Street, High Street and Castle Street assisted drainage of the heavy, though potentially fertile, boulder clay. This clay was a valuable resource for making pottery (8).

Alluvium deposited by the Mersey and the streams flowing into the Pool provided another ground surface in a few areas. Over the centuries it may have contributed to silting up the Pool which, during the medieval period, was tidal as far as the lower end of modern William Brown Street (9).

Liverpool before 1207

There is no firm evidence of settlement in Liverpool before the time of King John. Possible indications of prehistoric settlement are the Calderstones, located in nearby Allerton (1), and Bronze Age urns and flints discovered in Wavertree in the nineteenth century (2). Single finds of a stone axe and of flint arrowheads have been made in Wavertree and Childwall (3).

Since the nineteenth century it has been known that a Romano-British port existed at

Meols on the Wirral coast. Recent archaeological work in the wider Merseyside area has discovered other Romano-British settlements at Irby, Wirral, and along the line of the A5300 road in Halewood and Tarbock (4).

The nearest known Roman settlements are Chester and Wilderspool, Warrington. A few stray Roman coins have been found in Liverpool, but they could have been dropped at any date before their discovery: a sestertius of Trajan was found in Whitechapel (5); a coin of Antonius Pius came from the Harrington Street/North John Street junction (6); a third brass of Aurelian was dug up by Bridport Street (7); five Constantinian coins circa 320 AD were found in Tryon Street (8). Fragments of Roman pottery have been found in Roby and West Derby (9).

The only evidence for an Anglo-Saxon presence is a group of coins that is reported to have been found on the site of Exchange Station (10). There is no evidence for Vikings in Liverpool, although Viking-age stone sculpture is known at West Kirby and Bromborough (11).

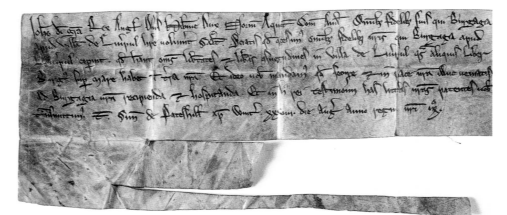

Translation:
"John by the grace of God King of England, Lord of Ireland, Duke of Normandy and Aquitane, Count of Anjou, to all his loyal subjects who may wish to have burgages in the township of Liverpul greeting. Know ye that we have granted to all our loyal subjects who shall take burgages in Liverpul that they shall have all the liberties and free customs in the township of Liverpul which any free borough on the sea has in our land. And therefore we command you that in safety and in our peace ye come thither to receive and occupy our burgages. And in testimony hereof we transmit to you these our letters patent. Witness Simon de Pateshill. At Winchester the 28th day of August in the 9th year of our reign [1207].

Figure 5: *King John's Letters Patent to Liverpool 28 August 1207.*

Liverpool is not mentioned by name in the Domesday Survey of 1086, but it is thought to have been one of the six unnamed berewicks (literally "barley farms"), or outliers attached to the important manor of West Derby. A coin of William I has been found in West Derby (12).

The name 'Liuerpul' first occurs in a charter dated between 1190 and 1194 that John, Count of Mortain (the future King John) issued to Henry, son of Warine de Lancaster. In it, John confirmed the grant by his father, King Henry II, to Warine of various places in South Lancashire (13); the original grant has not survived.

Historical Overview 1207-1770

In order to help the reader put sites into historical context a brief narrative of events that shaped Liverpool's development between 1207 and 1770 is given below. During the last 30 years archaeological work has increased our knowledge of Liverpool's past and brought its history to life. Detail of some of the work that has been done is included below and in the gazeteers where it is site specific.

Figure 6: *Excavation of a well in Chavasse Park 2004.*

Municipal and lordship

The borough

The Letters Patent of King John, commonly called the Charter, issued on 28th August 1207 established the borough of Liverpool. It offered settlers the opportunity of obtaining a burgage which comprised sufficient land for a house fronting the street and a long garden behind, an allocation of strips in the Townfield (see below), and common rights. It also granted exemption from various tolls and from forced agricultural service to a lord (to which inhabitants of manors were subject). Liverpool was created a privileged port, giving it exemption from certain dues and taxes. At its foundation Liverpool possessed around 150 burgesses, which had increased to 168 by 1296 (1). One of the principal attractions of burgage tenure was the freedom by which the plot could be sold, rented, devised or sub-divided without reference to the lord of the manor (2).

In 1229 King Henry III issued a new, fuller charter, on payment of ten marks by the burgesses, which became the governing charter of the borough for the next four hundred years. It established an independent borough for judicial purposes, gave the power to institute a merchant guild, and increased trading privileges. Liverpool had its first Member of Parliament by 1295 (3). Further charters issued from the thirteenth to the sixteenth centuries confirmed or clarified these rights (4).

In a thriving town such as Liverpool competition in trade led to intense pressure on burgage plots so by 1346 only 21 plots remained intact. The others had been divided into fractions as small as one forty-eighth. Conversely, the amalgamation of plots also took place and powerful Liverpool families such as the Moores exercised their right to consolidate holdings as large as 8 burgages. By 1379 over half the burgesses have occupations concerned with trade .

By the beginning of the seventeenth century Liverpool started to become more prosperous and agricultural interest in Liverpool's rural fringes had increased with the exploitation of the former Royal Park at Toxteth. In 1604 the Park was sold to the Molyneux family and conversion to arable and pasture land proceeded apace. However, the rights of the burgesses were somewhat uncertain and open to challenge, being based on vague medieval formulae which were increasingly open to debate. In 1626 the burgesses obtained a charter from Charles I which authorised the powers of the borough in more modern terms. It settled the constitution of the borough with a mayor, bailiffs and the burgesses as the supreme authority. Liverpool was made a 'body corporate and politic' with perpetual succession and giving it the right to set up a commercial court for the recovery of mercantile debts (5). It also confirmed control over the surrounding non-agricultural countryside (the waste) (6) and brought the legal system of the town into order.

After 1670 the town was extended over the Pool and new streets laid out on The Heath. A further step towards the city's independence was taken in 1699 when Liverpool became a port in its own right, having been under the jurisdiction of the port of Chester up to that time, and set up its own Customs house. Throughout the eighteenth century the business of the port and the powers of the municipality expanded together. The corporation was able to obtain Acts of Parliament and to raise the finance for major developments such as building the docks, expanding the road system, and erecting new churches (7). Liverpool Infirmary, a major new building funded by public subscription, was opened in 1749.

After 1770 there was a struggle between modernisers, who wished to grant a role in civic life to more inhabitants of the town, and traditionalists, who were satisfied with a system that permitted them to function as a self-perpetuating oligarchy. This was not resolved until the Reform Acts of the nineteenth century gave the vote to all adult males and similar developments in the twentieth century conferred the same rights on women.

The Townfield

The Townfield of Liverpool lay on the north of the medieval town. Stewart Brown (1916) has reconstructed it from medieval and later documents (8). The general position of most of the strips in the Townfield is known and they are indicated on the survey of Corporation property made by John Eyes in 1765.

The standard allocation was an acre in the open field, usually of 4 strips. The land in the open field was free of rent to the lord when sold separately from the burgage to which it was originally attached. The Townfield and Heath adjacent to Liverpool's seven streets encouraged a strong rural presence. Strips in the fields could be bought and transferred and could be used for arable and pastoral farming. The Heath to the east of the Pool supplied gorse for fuel and marl and clay as well as providing grazing land. Farming remained the sole occupation for a few men in seventeenth century Liverpool and a dual occupation for many.

By the end of the seventeenth century the Townfield is seldom mentioned. The creation of new external sources of trade and improvements in communications enabled Liverpool to grow away from its previous need for self-sufficiency. Together with a relaxation in rights, this gave the land owner freedom to do what he liked and to make money from his holding as he saw fit.

The bulk of the Townfield was enclosed in the eighteenth century and given over to new industry, for example in 1715 liberty was granted to towns people to get clay and marl for pot earth. By 1770 much of the remaining arable land had been relegated to grazing or market gardens (8).

Commerce and Trade

During the medieval period Chester was the main port serving the north west of England. Liverpool struggled to survive on domestic trade around the Irish Sea, with

Ireland being the mainstay of the town's commerce. There was some inland trade such as textiles bound for Manchester, but poor communications limited such activity. By the mid fifteenth century one or two ships per year traded with the Continent.

In the seventeenth century trade began to increase. Liverpool's low custom duties and the silting of the port at Chester contributed towards its growth. Salt from Cheshire was shipped from Liverpool to Lancashire coastal outlets and together with coal from the South Lancashire coal fields became the twin pillars of the town's commercial success (1). Liverpool was well-placed to take advantage of trade with new British colonies in the Americas. The first arrivals of tobacco and sugar from North America and the West Indies occurred in 1648 and 1666 respectively (2). The first sugar house was built by 1673.

By 1702, Liverpool had grown more rapidly than any port outside London, and 8600 tons of shipping was passing through the port (1). Salt exported from Liverpool was used in the Newfoundland cod fisheries, and also in Liverpool-based industries such as its potteries. Demand for coal grew as industries such as salt refining and glass-making developed in the town. The early eighteenth century expansion of merchant trade led to the construction of Liverpool's first wet dock, the first artificial wet dock in the world. A growing population of mariner-merchants was established in the town.

At the beginning of the eighteenth century local production was the norm for many English goods. However, as the century progressed, the development of better roads and the canal system, especially in Lancashire, improved communications and the transport of goods. In addition, new inventions transformed the county's industries. Much of the capital for the new canals was supplied by the wealth earned in the slave trade or the trade with the Americas. Liverpool's position, no more than a hundred miles from nearly all the districts most affected by the new inventions, permitted the town to profit from them (3).

The Docks

Until the end of the Stuart period the Pool of Liverpool provided shelter for ships that could reach the Town Quay at high tide. Vessels that could take the ground were able to lie close to the town. Deeper drafted vessels that had to lie in the Mersey were at the mercy of strong tidal currents and the wind and the weather. By the end of the seventeenth century ocean going ships sailing to Liverpool were finding the facilities inadequate.

By 1700, local merchants and members of the Town Council were actively seeking means to improve the situation and in 1710 the Corporation of Liverpool was in a position to commence the building of the world's first commercial wet dock with Thomas Steers as their engineer. Although the work was not fully complete, the new dock received its first ships on the 31 August 1715. Excavations by Oxford Archaeology North in 2001 showed that the dock wall survives extremely well. In places the wall top

Figure 7: *Archaeological work revealing the outline of St. George's Dock Basin 2006.*

is as much as 3.5 metres below modern ground level. The wall itself is still in very good condition, with two courses of large yellow sandstone blocks for a kerb, on top of courses of handmade bricks. On the north side of the dock organic deposits containing considerable amounts of worked timber were recovered (1).

The new Wet Dock was provided with an outer basin or Dry Dock and timber piers to assist ships entering and leaving the Wet Dock either side of high water. The Dock Act of 1737 provided for the enlargement of the Dry Dock (2) and the building of a new wet dock to the south but the work was slowed by political and financial difficulties. The New Pier forming the north west side of the enlarged Dry Dock and a graving dock at its northern end were completed about 1746 (3). Work on the new wet dock or South Dock, as it became known, did not start in earnest before 1750. It was open to shipping by 1754 (4).

A graving dock, also confusingly known as a dry dock, was built on the western side of the new entrance to South Dock in 1756. A further two graving docks were built on the western side of the Dry Dock between 1765 and 1769 and with later modifications, are still in existence.

The Dock Act of 1762 permitted the construction of a new wet dock and dry basin to the north of the Dry Dock. These became known as the North Dock or George's Dock and George's Dock Basin. The early works appear to have been entirely destroyed by a storm. A fresh start was made in 1767 when the mayor laid a foundation stone and the works were completed in 1771 (5). Remains of George's Dock Basin came to light during archaeological excavation in 2006.

The first wet dock eventually became known as the Old Dock, the Dry Dock after further alterations was named Canning Dock and South Dock assumed the popular name of Salthouse Dock.

By the eighteenth century Liverpool was trading with the whole of the known world apart from the Far East. The construction of each new dock fuelled the commercial pressure for further accommodation and the Dock Trustees had constantly to find ways of financing the enlargement of the Dock system.

Markets

It is not known where Liverpool's General Market was held before the Town Books begin to provide information from the mid sixteenth century. At that time (and probably from a lot earlier) it took place along Juggler Street (later High Street) between the High Cross at the Castle Street end and the White Cross at the top of Chapel Street. Saturday and Wednesdays were market days. The various products - foodstuffs, cloths, leather and similar household materials - were allotted to specific areas, for example the White Cross was long the site for potatoes.

Regulation of the Market was a personal responsibility of the Mayor. The Town Books reveal the continuous effort expended in keeping it honest and orderly. The main offences were attempts to circumvent the tolls on market goods charged to 'foreigners' at the entrances to the town; attempting to corner the market by buying up produce before it was displayed for sale; using unauthorised weights and measures and attempting to sell staples such as meat, fish, ale and bread that had spoiled. Each year two burgesses of the town were appointed as 'Levelookers' to supervise the market and to bring offenders before the Mayor's court.

During the later seventeenth century as the town grew the General Market is reported as spreading beyond its bounds and along Castle Street. At the start of the eighteenth century, when part of the Castle site was cleared, the opportunity was taken to move most of the General Market to the area. The Butcher's Shambles continued in High Street and the Corn Market remained in a widened Castle Street in front of the Town Hall (as shown on Chadwick's plan). After St George's Church was completed in 1734 the various parts of the General Market were provided with arcades and booths to its south side. For a while it was known as the Stocks Market until the nearby fixed Stocks and Pillory were removed.

In addition to the General Market there developed various other more specialised markets. From an early period cattle and swine from Ireland were landed at Liverpool ; a Cattle Market in Chapel Street is recorded in the late sixteenth century. By 1780 it had moved to St. James' Place, and then to Netherfield Road at the end of the century, reportedly because droves from Scotland had displaced Ireland as the primary source. A

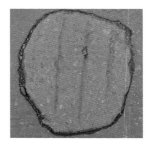

*Figure 8:*The Castle Street Sanctuary Stone in the roadway south of the Town Hall. The stone has been cut-off at its base.

Pig Market is reported in Prieston's Row off St James Street as shown on Perry's 1769 plan.

Cattle destined for Liverpool's meat supply were killed, prepared and displayed for sale in the Butcher's Shambles. While the original Shambles remained in a lane off High Street (now beneath Exchange Flags), increased demand in the spreading town led to additional ones being authorised in Dale Street and off Cable Street.

In the age of the horse, hay for fodder and bedding was required in great quantities. From before 1750 there was a Hay Market at the site of the present Old Haymarket outside the Birkenhead Tunnel entrance. By 1800 it had moved up St John's Lane to its junction with Lime Street.

Fish (especially salt fish) was a staple part of the diet of the town's poor. In the seventeenth century the Fish Market moved from Pool Lane to Chapel Street. In 1764 it was held at the top of Redcross Street and by 1784 it was at the bottom of St James Street. In 1792 a purpose built Doric columned hall was built for the Fish Market at the top of James Street where it remained for the next thirty years.

From the eighteenth century the site of the General Market became coveted for more profitable developments. Nothing came to fruition until early in the nineteenth century when the greens market was moved to Islington at the top of William Brown Street and St John's Market was built (1).

Fairs

In common with other medieval towns, Liverpool held a fair to serve both as a celebratory event and as an opportunity for travelling traders to offer goods for sale in Liverpool free of some of the usual restrictions on "foreign" tradespeople. The fair took place over three days from St Martin's Day in November. Later a second fair was staged in July. The extent of the fair was between the "liberty" or "sanctuary" stones set in Castle Street and Dale Street (1).

The fairs were opened with considerable ceremony by the Mayor attended by all his officials around the High Cross. A mayor's proclamation survives from 1637 enjoining the attendees to good behaviour and extending immunity from arrest for debt during the fair. This was apparently symbolised by a glove suspended from the High Cross. A bill for the food and drink provided for the Mayor's guests survives from 1775 (2).

Perhaps because the serious side of the fairs declined with the development of retail shops and to avoid disorder in its traditional central location these fairs ceased to be staged at the beginning of the nineteenth century. From before 1775 an alternative event, the Folly Fair, began to be held at Easter and Whitsuntide in fields and lanes in Islington at the top of Shaw's Brow (William Brown Street) and into London Road. This appears to have been a fun fair. It was apparently attended by extreme disorder and was stopped early in the nineteenth century (3).

Industry

Many industries such as milling and tanning would have been present in Liverpool since the medieval period but it is not until the seventeenth and eighteenth centuries that they become prominent in the historical record. During the eighteenth century several long-standing industries rose to their highest prosperity in the town. New industries such as sugar refining contributed to the town's commercial success. Summaries of the principal industries related to sites discussed in the gazetteers are given below.

Mills and Milling

Windmills, water mills and horse mills were all operated in Liverpool. Water mills and horse mills appear to have been established earlier than windmills and were placed nearer to the centre of town. The majority of windmills were placed on higher ground to the east and north-east of the town, such as Shaw's Brow (William Brown Street) and Limekiln Lane (Lime Street). The primary use of mills was for grinding foodstuffs such as grain, malt, beans and oil seeds. Another function was grinding minerals for industrial processes. Mills were also used as pumps to raise water from mines and other water-logged workings. William Moss in his 1796 guidebook attributes the large number of windmills in the town partly to the lack of a narrow fresh-water river suitable for driving watermills that most other towns had (1).

In many towns the corporation had the right to direct where mills could be erected and collect charges for milling. This was not the case in Liverpool because King John retained the legal right to milling when he gave a charter to the borough. Until the seventeenth century the Crown had a monopoly over mills. Other mills were erected when the authority of the Crown was weak, as in the 1530s. People sometimes took their flour to mills which were not authorised to grind the burgesses' flour, such as to the Castle mill in the 1660s. It was not until 1629 that King Charles I gave up his right and his successors were not able to enforce the monopoly (2).

In 1689, William Hands was granted a lease to erect a windmill which he could operate free of feudal duties. Within a few years many other windmills were erected on the ridge of high land that extended south from Townsend Mill and Eastham Windmill (3). In 1773, there were 27 mills in the town: 16 for grinding corn, 9 for grinding colours, one for rasping and grinding dyer's wood, and one for raising water at the salt works (4).

By 1835 most of the mills had gone out of use, or else had been converted to steam. Some appear on later maps as landmarks.

Figure 9: *The Sailors' Hospital and Liverpool Infirmary with Townsend Mill on the right.*

Salt

Liverpool's salt trade is first recorded in connection with the Moore's Salt House or Store in the seventeenth century. It seems likely that this was not a manufactory but received supplies from Cheshire's brine fields.

In 1670 the first rock salt mine opened near Northwich on the River Weaver. By the mid 1690s the Dungeon rock salt refinery had been established near Hale while in 1697 the Blackburne brothers opened a refinery in Liverpool beside the Strand inlet on the shore south of The Pool.

The new Salt Works brought together rock salt barged down the Weaver river with coal pack-horsed from Prescot. Typically the rock salt boilers produced 13 tons of fine table salt from 15 tons of rock salt dissolved and heated in 45 tons of river water (1).

Liverpool's proximity to sources of rock salt and coal enabled its salt exports to grow rapidly. The ability to carry rock salt overseas as ballast in ships engaged, for example, in the import of timber from the Baltic gave Liverpool's merchants a commercial advantage compared to rival ports. From 15,000 tons in 1732 exports of rock and refined salt reached over 150,000 tons by 1800.

This trade may not have equalled in value that of the sugar trade in powering the

rapid growth of Liverpool in the early eighteenth century, but after those rivals had declined in Liverpool, salt continued to provide the foundation of the salt based chemical industries of the nineteenth century.

Sugar Refining

In 1667-8 Sir Edward Moore leased a croft off Dale Street to Allyn Smith, a London sugar baker, who planned to build a sugar refinery. However, sugar refining in Liverpool began when Richard Cleaveland and Dan Danvers built the first sugar house, a five storey building, between 1670 and 1673 (1). By 1768 there were 8 sugar houses. Seven of these are shown on George Perry's map of 1769. In 1704, some 27 years after the start of the industry in Liverpool, only 760 tons of raw sugar was imported through the port. By 1785 this had risen to 16,600 tons shared between up to a dozen sugar houses. Liverpool's sugar refining industry was made possible by the West Indian trade, and grew with the port. The sugar trade continued to increase after the abolition of slavery, and into the latter half of the twentieth century (2).

Tanning

It is likely that tanning was practised in Liverpool as a by-product of stock farming from the earliest years of the town. The first record of the tanning industry in Liverpool is from early in the reign of Queen Elizabeth I, when John Smith was involved in a ten-year dispute with his neighbour in Castle Street over the stench caused by his tanning and lime pits (1). Tanneries and other noxious industries were generally located on the outskirts of the town, as can be seen by comparison of eighteenth and early nineteenth century Liverpool maps.

Pottery

Pottery was produced in south west Lancashire during the Medieval period (1) but evidence for earthenware manufacture in Liverpool is not found until early in the eighteenth century, when Samuel Shaw established a pottery on the slope of the hill which became known as Shaw's Brow (William Brown Street). The early Liverpool pottery was of the Dutch type of tin-glazed earthenware, with a coarse body and thick white or blue glaze, commonly known as Delft.

By 1766 there were six potteries in Shaw's Brow, and a further eight potters in the town, including Alderman Thomas Shaw, the son of Samuel, whose pottery was in Dale Street, and Richard Chaffers, a successful early porcelain manufacturer. The Pennington family (Seth, John, and James) all owned potteries, and Philip Christian was an important Liverpool potter. William Reid's china factory (1756-61) was excavated by archaeologists from National Museums Liverpool in 1997-98. The excavations

Figure 10: *Excavations at Manchester Dock in 2007 reveal the remains of late eighteenth or early nineteenth century sugar moulds which would have been used in the refining process to make sugar loaves.*

Figure 11: *A pottery in Shaw's Brow.*

recovered large quantities of kiln brick, saggar and other kiln furniture and many tiny fragments of biscuit ware and porcelain (2).

Liverpool potteries declined in the late eighteenth century and were unable to compete successfully with Staffordshire potteries. All except the Herculaneum Pottery, founded 1796, disappeared in the early nineteenth century (3).

Glass Manufacture

The first glass manufactory in Liverpool was opened by Mr. Josiah Poole in 1715, and was operated under several different owners until at least 1781. The 'New' glasshouse in South Dock was built in 1759, and was still operational in 1779, but had closed by 1803. In addition, a short-lived glasshouse making fine flint glass operated in Dale Street from 1756 to about 1761. The evident lack of profitability of glass making in Liverpool in the latter part of the eighteenth century is consistent with the rise in specialised centres for production. St. Helens' growth as a glass making centre paralleled Liverpool's expansion as a major port, and glass-making in Liverpool also faced local competition from Warrington and Prescot (1).

Silk Manufacture

The growth of silk cloth manufacture in eighteenth century England was strongly encouraged. High tariffs were levied on imports of fully-manufactured silk items. When total prohibition was imposed from 1765 to 1826, restrictions were placed on the import of silk thread also. Lancashire, Cheshire, and Staffordshire were major English silk manufacturing areas, alongside London and Dorset. Liverpool had two silk houses in 1769, one a weaving house and the other a throwster's house producing silk thread. During the Napoleonic Wars, when Britain was at war with the leading European silk producing nation of France, the British silk manufacturing industry received strong government protection (1).

Brewing and Distilling

The earliest recorded brewer in Liverpool was one William Furnival, who, as well as being a brewer around 1680, was also an innkeeper and churchwarden residing in Water Street. From this time on the names of other brewers appear in the records and some of the earliest are Henry Mercer of Water Street, William Denton of Water Street, John Scarisbrick of Moor Street and Adam Atkinson of Lord Street (1).

Brewing was carried out mainly for home consumption. Gore's Directory for 1766 contains entries for thirty eight brewers, most of whom were probably inn-keepers who brewed their own wares (2). In 1773 there were 36 breweries in Liverpool, 33 for home consumption, which might encompass retail sale in an inn, and 3 for export (3).

Rope manufacture

A thriving port consumed, through wear and tear, vast quantities of spars, sails, and ropes. The shipwright's yards, sail lofts and rope walks have long gone from Liverpool but the latter at least have left an indelible mark upon the present city's street plan.

The anchor cables of a large sailing ship were ropes of up to 16 inches (40 centimetres) in circumference, 1000 feet (300 metres) in length, and weighing more than a ton. Spinning together smaller ropes to make a larger one was demanding in power and space. A Ropery or Rope Walk was typically a narrow, straight and level stretch of ground up to several hundred metres in length with an engine and spinning machinery housed at one end.

The Chadwick plan of 1725 shows three walks on the east and south edges of the town. This had quadrupled by 1765. Most were in the less productive land to the east and south outside the built-up area of the town. By 1785 new developments had spread over half of the sites. This change probably reflects not a fall in demand but rising land values that had swept the rope makers "off the map" to cheaper fields elsewhere.

Disputes occurred between the rope makers and developers eager to lay out streets

Figure 12: *A view of Liverpool from Copperas Hill showing a Rope Works in the foreground.*

across their walks. A notable example occurred in the seventeenth century when Sir Edward Moore was forced to bridge over his tenant William Bushell's rope walk to complete Fenwick Street (see gazetteer entry for the Dry Bridge) (1). Newington, between Renshaw Street and Bold Street, also bridged a rope walk.

A number of modern streets echo the line of rope-walks including Cable Street, Bold Street and Berry Street while Renshaw Street and Duke Street were built alongside former walks. In the nineteenth century railway lines approaching Central Station took over the rope walk beneath Newington. The former Ropery on Skelhorne Street was only altered with the construction of the south 'shed' at Lime Street Station in the nineteenth century. It could be claimed that the whole pattern of the present streets between Renshaw Street and Duke Street (the site of the twenty first century Ropewalks Quarter) had been laid out by the Georgian rope industry.

Places of Worship and Crosses

There is no record of any places of worship in Liverpool before 1207. Within fifty years the first Christian chapel, St Mary del Kay, had been built by the river shore. The second chapel to be built, one hundred years later in 1356, was St Nicholas, in the same area at the river end of what is now Chapel Street. Liverpool was part of the parish of St Mary at Walton until 1699 when it became a parish in its own right and consequently no other church is recorded until the beginning of the eighteenth century. No monasteries, convents or friaries are recorded; the nearest known ones were at Birkenhead, Norton, Stanlow and Chester across the Mersey, and Warrington and Burscough in Lancashire. Wayside markers in the form of crosses were set up on the roads leading into the town, and other crosses in the town centre functioned as places for gathering, proclamation and selling goods.

As part of the Tudor reformation of the church in England, St Mary del Kay was closed in 1548, and in 1553 it was seized by the King's Commissioners and sold to Liverpool Corporation. St Nicholas's chapel became the only place of worship for the next 150 years. During this period there was a growth in Protestantism in the town, in contrast to the many Catholic land-owners in the surrounding countryside. As early as 1685 protestant Huguenot refugees from France were harboured in the town's workhouses and encouraged to work (1). On her visit to Liverpool in 1699 the traveller Celia Fiennes remarked on the large number of dissenters.

After the parish of Liverpool was established in 1699, there was a great spurt of church building. Between 1700 and 1769 Acts of Parliament were obtained to build the Anglican churches of St Peter's on Church Street, St George's on the site of the Castle in Derby Square, St Thomas's on Park Lane and St Paul's in St Paul's Square (remains of St Paul's Church came to light during the course of archaeological work in 2005). During the same period a number of non-conformist chapels were built for congregations of Baptists, Methodists, Quakers, and Dissenters variously described as Presbyterians or Unitarians. This is an indication both of increased tolerance of dissenting religious views by the Anglican establishment and of the expanding population of the town. One near-contemporary observer, Richard Brooke, noted that the churches were built of stone and the chapels of brick (2), which suggests the greater wealth of the Anglicans. Roman Catholics opened places of worship in discreet locations, as their chapels were illegal and in danger of being attacked by anti-Catholic groups. The first Jewish meeting-place is believed to have been established by German Jews in the middle of the eighteenth century.

The surge of church and chapel-building continued throughout the last quarter of the eighteenth century and into the nineteenth century. Unfortunately, all the churches and chapels alluded to above have been closed down and the buildings destroyed, except for

St Paul's Church; inset - the foundations are revealed during archaeological investigation in 2005.

Benn's Garden Presbyterian Chapel, one of the earliest Dissenters' Chapels in eighteenth century Liverpool.

St Nicholas' Church whose foundation dates back to the fourteenth century but none of the original structure survives.

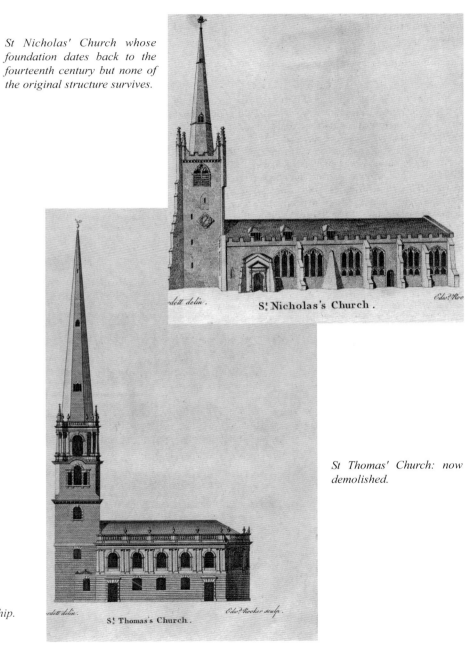

St Thomas' Church: now demolished.

Figure 13: *Liverpool places of worship.*

Figure 14: St. Peter's Church about 1920, originally consecrated in 1704. The church held the town's first library. Inset: a cross set in the pavement in Church Street marks the site.

one. The survivor is the church of St Nicholas, which has existed for over 650 years on the same site, although the present building was rebuilt after bomb damage in the Second World War.

Charitable Institutions

Schools

Grammar school education in Liverpool began with the establishment of a Grammar School in 1515 to be conducted in the 'Chapel of St Mary del Key' and financed by a bequest from the will of John Crosse, Rector of St Nicholas Fleshambles, London (1). This early Free Grammar School survived until the eighteenth century and was taken down in 1745 (2). In 1613 another Grammar School was founded at Walton on the Hill, four miles away (3).

The Bluecoat School (1709 - present) was established as a charity school on a plot of

land, bounded by Schoolhouse Lane, Hanover Street, College Lane and Peter Street (4). The instigator and major benefactor of the project was Bryan Blundell, merchant, mariner and ship owner, who had made his wealth trading with the West Indies and Virginia. He was said to be greatly distressed by the sight of ragged children in the streets of Liverpool (5). Initially a simple day school was built by subscription for 40 boys and 10 girls who were 'provided with cloaths and learning', but by 1714 numbers had increased so much that a new school where 'the children might live under regular discipline' was begun (6). According to Enfield (7) the children worked in the school and were engaged in spinning cotton.

Another charity school developed by the early 1700s out of the collapse of the old Liverpool Grammar School. In 1721 the Mayor visited this 'Free School,' which had once stood in the Old Church Yard of St Nicholas but had moved to School Lane (8). It became known as the 'Free Grammar School' and survived until 1803 (9). Despite its name, the presence of a 'Stocking Manufactory' above the school suggests it might have provided vocational training .

The education of girls was a matter for consideration. Some of the girls from the Bluecoat School were, in the 1750s, apprenticed to female businesswomen, notably a draper, a mantua-maker and a biscuit-maker (10). Gore's Directory listed in 1766 two schools in Liverpool under the names of women who might have been the proprietors (11).

The expanding economy of eighteenth century Liverpool, needed a vocational and commercial education rather than one based on the Classics. It is notable that some of the independent schools of the time were meeting this need, such as William Smith's school in Redcross Street, where the curriculum set out by his son, Egerton Smith, offered "writing, arithmetic, merchants' accounts, navigation, geography and the use of the globes, maps, charts, planisphere, the rudiments of astronomy, geometry etc." (12). This kind of curriculum was being developed outside the grammar school tradition by non-conformist schools. A Dissenting Academy was founded in nearby Warrington, where Joseph Priestly taught for a number of years.

Later in the eighteenth century, concern for the religious needs of poor children led to the organization of a movement in 1784 for the development of Sunday Schools for the Poor. The first Sunday School was set up in 1789 in the Old Church School Moorfields, followed in 1790 by Unitarian Schools in Mount Pleasant and the Wesleyan School, Brunswick (13). It became fashionable for the townsfolk of Liverpool to watch the Sunday procession to St Peter's Church of the Bluecoat Boys and Girls (14). Religious toleration was a feature of Liverpool (15) evident in both philanthropic and educational ventures. One such example was the establishment in 1825 of the North and South Corporation Schools, where Protestants and Catholics were for a time educated side by side (16).

Philanthropy combined with commercial good sense in the setting up, in 1791, of a School for the Indigent Blind which aimed "to furnish them (the blind) with some

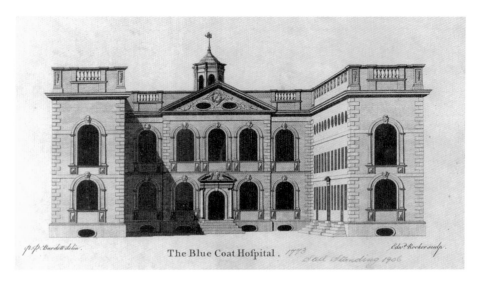

Figure 15: *The Bluecoat Hospital as it appeared around 1770.*

employment which may prevent them from being burdens to their family and the community". The School also aimed to "engage the mind" and provide a "portion of religious knowledge as may reconcile them to their situation" (17).

The establishment of the Royal Institution in Colquitt Street in 1817 was the first step towards the development of Higher Education in Liverpool, followed in 1834 by the Medical School, which laid the real foundations for the establishment of a University College in Liverpool (18).

Almshouses and Workhouses

The earliest record in Liverpool of a poor house, also known as Pool House or a House of Correction, is from 1557-8, which described a small square building situated at the foot of Pool Lane (1), now beneath the Law Courts. Initially it was used for the care of the poor and the sick (2). It has been suggested that it might have been used also as the ferry house of the priory on the south side of the river (3). Pool Lane, near the waterfront, was noted as being a rough area of the town (4) so by 1598 it was hired from the then owner Robert Moore, as a 'house of correction' for the poor (5). A rental of 1668 has a similar record (6). Pool House survived until 1804 when it was demolished (7).

In the late seventeenth and early eighteenth centuries three groups of almshouses were built at the end of Dale Street and Shaw's Brow (William Brown Street). The first almshouses were thought to be founded by the benefactor David Poole in 1684 (8).

They were followed in 1692 by Dr Sylvester Richmond's foundation for the widows of sailors, and in 1724 by Scarsbrick's Almshouses, both set up as a sort of annexe to Poole's (9). The generosity of these benefactions reflects not only the philanthropic attitudes of the time, but also the needs of a growing commercial seaport.

These almshouses served their turn, but by the mid eighteenth century they were dilapidated and regarded as obstructions to new developments in the area. In 1735 the central block was pulled down to increase the flow of traffic northwards, and in 1748 they were demolished and a new set of almshouses was built on the south east corner of St John's Lane fronting Lime Street (10).

A fourth group of almshouses situated at the junction of Bold Street and Hanover Street was endowed by Richard Warbrick in 1706 for sailors' widows. They were demolished in 1787 along with the new ones situated at the Fall Well (11). A new almshouse or House of Industry was built at the Junction of Cambridge Street and Arrad Street at the top of 'Martindale's Hill', described as a healthy, open situation, in 1788 (12). By the early twentieth century this institution was demolished in turn and replaced by a Maternity Hospital which, according to the date stone, was opened in 1926. This was superseded at the end of the twentieth century by the present Students' Residences for the University of Liverpool.

Yet another poor house existed on the south side of the Bluecoat School on the corner of College Lane and Hanover Street, which is described by Enfield as the "first appearance of a poor house in Liverpool in 1723" (13). This poor house was abandoned in 1770 when the workhouse on Brownlow Hill was built. In addition to providing work for the inmates, a separate fever hospital existed, staffed in 1865 by twelve nurses trained at the Nightingale School. This workhouse, the largest in England, survived until 1931 and was considered in its time to be strictly, but well, run (14).

The importance to Liverpool of its seafarers was not forgotten during this period of rebuilding. In 1749 a 'Hospital' was attached to the newly-built Liverpool Infirmary. Often called the 'Sixpenny Hospital' (15), this institution provided care, once again, for "decayed seamen, their widows and children" (16).

Law and Order

Early in its history Liverpool struggled against its overlords for control of Manorial Court powers in the borough. Eventually it was successful with its Port Moot Court securing equivalent authority under the superior Duchy Court at the county seat of Lancaster. Responsibility for law and order in Liverpool rested with the Mayor, the town's chief citizen and Chairman of the Court. Sometimes a knight or peer but invariably a gentleman, the Mayor was usually chosen from the powerful merchants of the town. Through their representation on the Town's Common Council the merchants passed bylaws for ordering the affairs of the Town, Port and Market that were enforced

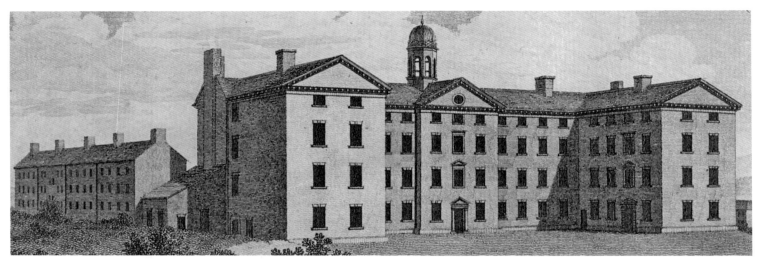

Figure 16: *Liverpool Poor House in 1773.*

Figure 17: *Cambridge Street Alms Houses.*

through the Port Moot Court. Later in the seventeenth century the court became known as the Court of Passage.

The Recorder, usually a lawyer, advised the Mayor. To enforce his authority the Mayor had a Serjeant at Mace with powers of arrest and two Bailiffs responsible for enforcing judgements in the Town and Market. Up to the nineteenth century the court also controlled the port and a Water Bailiff had powers of arrest and enforcement over shipping in the Mersey and its approaches. All burgesses of the town were sworn to assist the Serjeant and Bailiffs if 'deputised'. These were not popular duties, not infrequently the officers were injured and sometimes themselves charged and fined for shirking! The Bailiffs kept the town's arms and the Mayor could call in emergencies upon a band of burgesses trained as soldiers. Ten musketeers and ten pikesmen are recorded in 1625 (1).

Alongside the market tolls and the port customs, the fines collected through the Mayor's Court provided a significant part of the early borough's revenues. Fines not paid became debts so the early Town Hall provided space for remanding the accused waiting to go before the Mayor and for imprisoning debtors until their family had paid the fines. When the Old Tower became available as a gaol debtors were also held there but those of quality remained for a further period in the Town Hall. Failure to discharge a debt could lead to the debtor being pressed into indentured service with one of the town's leading merchants.

Keeping order became more difficult as the town and port grew rapidly in the eighteenth century. As conditions became bleaker for the poor, deference and acceptance of the established order declined. Whilst in earlier times a couple of night watchmen were sufficient, the records show the appointment of increasing numbers of constables to help keep order, from four in 1718 to fourteen in 1750 (2). The bridewells served them as bases and as overnight lockups for the drunk and disorderly.

Early in the eighteenth century the Mayor and Recorder became magistrates in the lower criminal court and retired mayors automatically became coroners. Those held on felony charges were sent to Lancaster for sentence; if they escaped death or transportation, they were returned to the Old Tower to serve their sentence at Liverpool's expense. Lesser criminal acts, misdemeanors, fell within the remit of the Mayor's Quarter Sessions. Sentences included prison, fines, whipping, the pillory or stocks, and providing sureties. Excavations in the 1970s in South Castle Street area revealed the remains of what are believed to be the pillory and the cage (lock-up). A short sentence working in the House of Correction was deemed suitable mainly for poorer offenders, for offences such as vagrancy and disorderly or lewd conduct. For the better off, fines sometimes combined with assurances for future conduct were the preferred sentence.

At the end of the eighteenth century penal reformers began to argue that prison could perhaps reform felons if combined with either hard labour or solitary confinement. New prisons were built with some state aid, often designed on "scientific principles" as was Liverpool's New Borough Goal built in Great Howard St in the 1780s. By the end of the century the town had been divided into wards each assigned with several constables and the ground was laid for the development of an organised police force.

Communications

Of Liverpool's earliest streets, Chapel Street and Moor Street (Tithebarn Street) led out to the Townfield and beyond to Walton. From there the road to the North (the "Scotland Road") developed through Ormskirk to the Ribble crossing at Preston and so to the county seat of the Duchy of Lancashire at Lancaster. Bank Street (Water Street) and Dale Street ran to the dale at the head of the Pool. An important road developed eastwards from here across the Great Heath towards the seats of the powerful Molyneux and Stanley families at Croxteth and Knowsley. The "London Road" developed through Prescot to link with the national route south at the Mersey crossing at Warrington. The streets mentioned above were intersected by the line of Castle Street, Juggler Street (High Street) and Whitecross Street (Old Hall Street). These very early streets, together with various crosslinks and lanes, were sufficient almost until the first dock was built and the upper Pool reclaimed.

Liverpool's first road developments may have reflected the interests of the powerful but from the sixteenth century the demands of commerce predominated such as Manchester's trade with Ireland through the port. Due to poor navigability in the upper Mersey system most of the traffic, Lancashire cloths and manufactured goods to be exchanged for Irish yarns, was pack horsed to and from Liverpool. In order to improve the flow, as strings of 60 or 70 left Liverpool daily, the road

Figure 18: *Liverpool in 1715 looking towards the river.*

through Prescot was 'causeyed', that is, laid with slabs just wide enough for pack horses to pass.

Liverpool's own industries demanded increasing supplies of coal. The town was fortunate in having productive mines of high quality coal nearby at Wigan and Prescot. By the middle of the 18th century the roads, though widened, were breaking down under the weight of many unsprung coal waggons. The responsibility for maintenance of county roads rested on the parishes and townships through which they passed. The work was undertaken under a supervisor appointed by the local magistrate using carts and labour extorted from parishioners. This semi-voluntary system was soon inadequate to deal with the increased traffic.

Liverpool's mayor and leading merchants combined to apply the turnpike system to the problem. This transferred making and maintaining a road to Trustees, financed by the capitalists who would benefit most and be repaid by the right to charge tolls. An Act covering the vital Liverpool to Prescot stage was secured in 1726. The system was extended to Manchester via Warrington and to Preston via Wigan by 1753. The Scotland road from Liverpool to Preston via Ormskirk had been turnpiked by 1771.

Until the eighteenth century individual long distance travel usually meant passage on a carrier's goods waggon or in a private coach. From about 1725 the well-off had the additional choice of riding to Warrington to join an established stage coach route going north or south. By about 1750 there was a regular coach service between Liverpool and Manchester and from about 1765 a regular service to London. Initially the London service made the journey in about four days with frequent changes of horse teams but as the roads improved into the nineteenth century more specialised coaches reduced the time to less than 48 hours at a considerably higher fare.

Much attention was paid to schemes to improve navigation in the rivers between Liverpool and Manchester. The first works of deepening and straightening the river channels were authorised in 1720. Other improvements followed but the route was not fully developed until the completion of the Bridgewater Canal in 1774. From the 1730s similar improvements to the Douglas stream from Wigan and to the Weaver river above Runcorn speeded the flow of coal and of rock salt to Liverpool industries. In 1767 designs were presented for a major canal from Liverpool to Yorkshire. Once again Liverpool promoters were prominent and it was due to the impetus they provided that the section of the Leeds to Liverpool Canal, of prime benefit to their interests, was completed to the Wigan coalfields by 1774.

How to use the gazetteers
The main body of the book is divided into four chapters covering 1207-1539 (Medieval which also covers the Early Tudor period), 1540-1659 (Tudor, Early Stuart and Commonwealth), 1660-1713 (Later Stuart period) and 1714-1770 (George I - George III). There is a plan of modern day Liverpool which enables the readers to orientate themselves in the twenty first century city.

For each of the four periods there is a plan (sketch map) of the town as it was in that period, with sites marked. The accompanying gazetteers (tables) give information about all the sites that we know about, including some that are not shown on the plans because their exact location is not known. Some sites are not shown because they were situated some way from the heart of the old town so they do not appear on original maps.

Every site has a unique number that identifies it on all the plans and in all the gazetteers, for example the Castle is site 1. Sites which fell out of use in the earlier periods are mentioned in gazetteers for later periods but are not shown on the corresponding plans, for example Eastham Dale Water Mill, site 10, is mentioned in all gazetteers but is not shown on the Later Stuart or George I-George III plans.

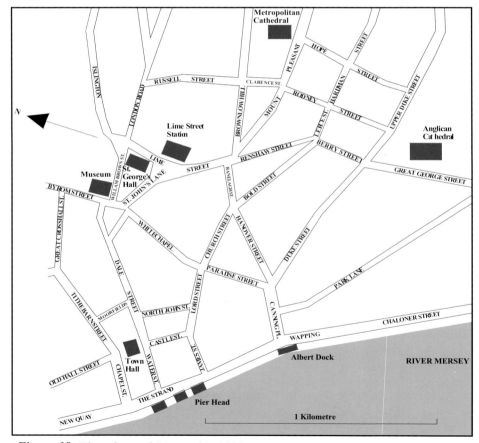

Figure 19: *Plan of central Liverpool in 2007.*

Medieval: 1207-1539

On 28th August 1207, King John, issued the Letters Patent (charter) which established Liverpool as a borough (1). Although the document refers to the land or township of Liverpool, it does not refer to any pre-existing settlement, but it is likely that there were some dwellings there before 1207. The charter offered settlers the opportunity of obtaining a burgage (2), and in return, the burgess (holder of a burgage plot) was obliged to pay one shilling a year for their holding and to appear at the Courts (3).

From the start Liverpool was a planned town. Seven streets were laid out in an H shape extending along the spine and sloping sides of the peninsula. The original streets are Water Street, Castle Street, Chapel Street, Dale Street, High Street, Tithebarn Street and Old Hall Street. The earliest documentary evidence for most of these is around 1300 (4). Some of the streets have changed their names at least once. High Street was formerly Juggler Street and Tithebarn Street was previously called Moor Street. The name Bank Street was in use for Water Street up to 1594 (5) although it was also called by its present name from 1540-1 (6). There was a Whiteacre Street up to 1539 (7), but later it was absorbed into Mill Street, which had been re-named Old Hall Street by 1629 (8). They have all survived up to the present day.

The first significant buildings were constructed of stone. Liverpool Castle was built round about 1235 by William de Ferrers. The first chapel, dedicated to St. Mary del Key (Quay) was built in the early thirteenth century and the Chapel of St. Nicholas in 1355/6; both were chapels of ease, not parish churches, because Liverpool was part of the parish of St. Mary at Walton-on-the-Hill until 1699. The Moores erected Moore Hall in the 13th century; and the Stanleys had a house from 1252, which was fortified as the Tower some time before 1406. By the beginning of the sixteenth century the Crosse family had built Crosse Hall (which gave its name to Crosshall Street).

In 1515 John Crosse bequeathed the first Town Hall to the Mayor and Corporation. The upper room was used as court room, guild meeting place and prison for freemen with, underneath it, the town warehouse, custom house and prison.

The earliest commercial buildings known are the Priory of Birkenhead's granary in the Bank Street/Chapel Street area (9) and the Molyneux family's tithe barn in Moor Street, which gave rise to its new name of Tithebarn Street. It is not known what the first port constructions, such as wharfs or warehouses, looked like. A ferry is first mentioned in 1256 (10). Three mills existed for grinding corn by 1256. Pottery manufacture is first recorded in the early fourteenth century (11).

The land around the town was cultivated as two or three large open fields, the Townfield, shared by burgessess and others, such as the Prior of Birkenhead (12). The fields were divided into sections ('shots') each containing strips of earth for ploughing ('butts', 'lands' or 'selions') separated by narrow, unploughed bands ('balks'), and the sections were allocated to individuals. Saltons Moor, on the Kirkdale boundary, was brought into cultivation in the 14th century (13). The Great Heath and the Moss were valuable for grazing and fuel, and came gradually under the control of the burgesses (14).

No firm figures for population are known for this period. The initial settlers may have numbered around 150 families, rising to 168 in 1296, and 196 by 1346, but this dropped to 86 by 1379, probably as a result of the Black Death (15). The main occupations of the inhabitants were farming, fishing and trade.

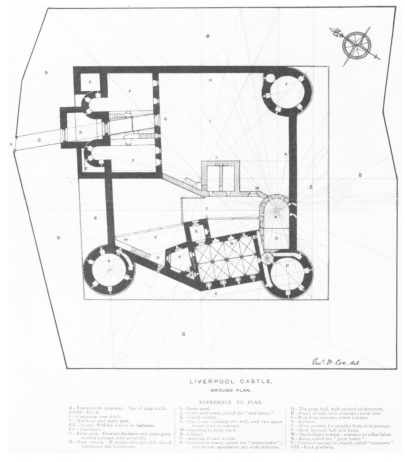

LIVERPOOL CASTLE.
GROUND PLAN.

REFERENCE TO PLAN.

Figure 20: *A Victorian reconstruction of the 1442 ground plan of Liverpool Castle based on original documents (after Edward Cox).*

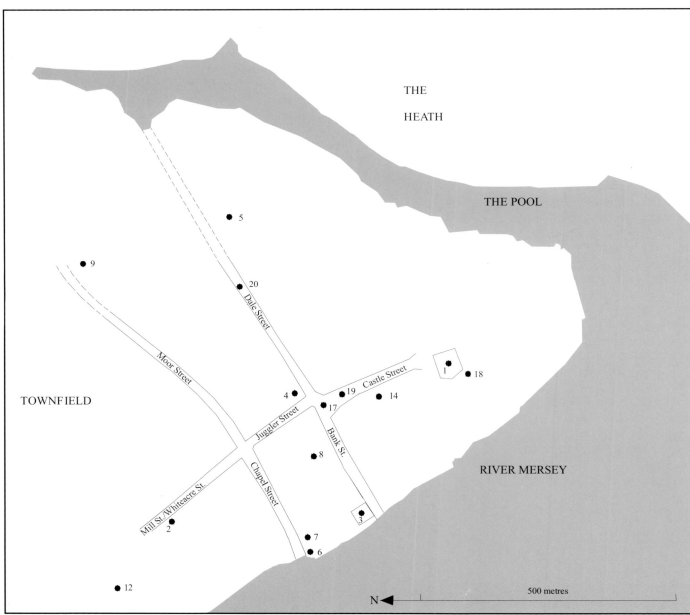

Key:
1. Castle
2. Old (Moore) Hall
3. Tower
4. Town Hall
5. Crosse Hall

Places of Worship
6. St Mary del Key Chapel
7. St Nicholas' Chapel

Commerce and Industry
8. Granary
9. Tithe barn
12. Horse Mill
14. Horse Mill

Crosses
Wayside Crosses
17. The High Cross
18. Red Cross

Sanctuary Stones
19. Castle Street
20. Dale Street

The following entries in the gazetteer are not shown on the plan:
10, 11, 13, 15, 16

Figure 21: Plan of Medieval Liverpool 1207 - 1539.

Medieval Gazetteer

Name	Location	Description
1. Castle	Derby Square (OS:SJ34269027).	Built on rock circa 1235 by William de Ferrers (1) and moated (2). Turreted curtain walls connected four towers enclosing a courtyard which by 1347 contained a hall, chapel, brewhouse, bakehouse and a covered well (3). A drawbridge and gatehouse on the north side formed the main entrance (4). An underground passage from the north west corner ran to the shore (5). An apple orchard was on the west (6) and a stone built dovecot to the south (7). The first recorded repairs were in 1323 to prepare for Edward II's visit (8). In 1400-61 there were general repairs to defences, a new bakehouse was built while in 1441 the south east tower was built or repaired (9). Further repairs were ordered in 1476 (10).
2. Old (Moore) Hall	Under Old Hall Street and Liverpool Echo Building (OS:SJ33999072).	Home of the Moore family after they settled in Liverpool in the 13th century (11). Moore Hall became known as Old Hall and was used as the dower house after Thomas Moore built Bank Hall, Kirkdale, in 1388-9 on land acquired in 1280 (12).
3. Tower	North side of lower end of Water Street (OS:SJ34009038).	In 1406 Henry IV granted Sir John Stanley a licence to embattle his stone built house close to the sea (13). Attached smaller buildings occupied three sides of a courtyard with the Tower, with gardens to the north and east, according to Picton, who based this description partly on Perry's plan of 1769 (14). The Stanleys became Earls of Derby in 1485 after their service to Henry VII at the Battle of Bosworth.
4. Town Hall	East side of High Street near junction with Dale Street (OS:SJ34219050).	In 1511 the 'gilde house' and 'courte house' are referred to. The building was probably the one bequeathed by John Crosse in 1515 to the Mayor, Aldermen and burgesses, but it may formerly have been town property which had somehow come into the Crosses' possession (15). The Hall was used as court room, guild meeting place and prison for freemen with, underneath it, the town warehouse, custom house and prison for common criminals and others. The upper room, roofed with stone slates, was reached by an outside flight of stone steps.
5. Crosse Hall	Site of Municipal Buildings, south side of Dale Street (OS:SJ34589067).	Home of the Crosse family, the house is first mentioned in documents in 1520 (16). The estate extended as far as the edge of the Pool on the south and east (17).

Medieval Gazetteer

Name	Location	Description
Places of Worship		
6. St Mary del Key Chapel	South side of lower end of Chapel Street (OS:SJ33939048).	The stone-built chapel was erected on rock above the sea shore before 1257 (18). Two chantries were endowed about 1353-60 (19). Its upkeep is referred to in 1456 and 1459, and in 1464 land in Garston was granted to maintain it (20). In 1515, by the will of John Crosse, a London clergyman, the priests were to open a grammar school (21).
7. St Nicholas' Chapel	South side of lower end of Chapel Street, inland from St Mary del Key (OS:SJ33979047).	The chapel was begun in 1355 and was consecrated in 1361 with its adjoining cemetery (22). It had a nave, a north aisle and a square tower at the west end (23). John of Gaunt endowed a chantry at the main altar in 1361 (24).
Commerce and Industry		
8. Granary	Near the Water Street end of Rumford Street area (OS: SJ341-904-).	This belonged to Birkenhead Priory who owned the site from before circa 1300; the Priory also held land in Liverpool town fields (25). The granary was sold after the dissolution of the Priory in 1536 and bought by the Moore family (26). In 1668 Sir Edward Moore described a pair of stone steps at the back of the building that had led to an upper room, where, at the end of each market day, the monastic corn which had remained unsold was stored until the following market day.
9. Tithe barn	Close to the junction of Marybone and Great Crosshall Street (OS: SJ344- 009-).	A stone building erected in 1523-4 by Sir William Molyneux. The tithes of Walton parish had been given to Shrewsbury Abbey in the late eleventh century, and were sold by the Abbey to the Molyneux family in the fifteenth century (27).
10. Eastham Dale Water Mill	Close to site of John Moores University, Byrom Street campus (OS:SJ348-911-).	A watermill, first mentioned in 1256, was situated in Eastham Dale beside a dammed stream flowing from the Moss Lake towards the head of the Pool (28). There is a later reference in 1423 (29). A second watermill is mentioned in 1256 and in 1423 but it cannot be located. The Eastham Dale mill pool was shown in a 1720 sketch map which showed a diminished Eastham Brook still running towards "Eastyn Myll Dam". A small pool is shown on maps of 1790 and 1807 (30).
11. Eastham Wind Mill	On high ground north west of junction of Gerard Street and Christian Street (OS: SJ349-910-).	From 1256 there are frequent references to this mill which, like the Eastham Dale watermill, belonged to the Crown. It was leased to various tenants including the Moore and Crosse families (31). The windmill was repaired in 1450 for 4s 7d; the annual rent then was 26s 8d (32).

Medieval Gazetteer

Name	Location	Description
12. Horse Mill (1)	North west of Old Moore Hall in an area west of Old Hall Street and north of Union Street (OS:SJ338-907-).	In use by 1322, it replaced a watermill (33). It was used for grinding malt for the Moores' tenants. Part of Whiteacre Street (Old Hall Street) was renamed Mill Street (34). The Mill was still used up to 1531 (35).
13. Townsend Mill	On the site of the Steble fountain in front of the Walker Art Gallery (OS:SJ35009074).	This was a wooden post-mill recorded from 1347. Like the Eastham wind and water mills it was Crown property and was leased with them, or separately. The Moores usually held Townsend Mill. When it was rebuilt in 1450, the annual rent was 13s 4d (36). It was also known as Nebb Mill (37).
14. Horse Mill (2)	Near south corner of junction of Brunswick Street and Castle Street (OS:SJ34229036).	This mill was set up by William Moore at some time before 1531. It was more centrally placed than the other horse mill beyond the Old Hall. Other horse mills were in use, but they cannot be located (38).

Crosses
Wayside Crosses

Name	Location	Description
15. Everston Cross	West side of Bevington Hill above the north slip road from Kingsway Tunnel to Scotland Road (OS:SJ347-917-).	This was close to the southern limit of the Breckshoots section of the Townfield. First mentioned circa 1300 (39) it was referred to frequently as a landmark. It was also called the Little Cross and Overston Cross (40). Although it is not named, there are two references to strips of land 'between the Crosses', one in 1490, and one in 1508 (41).
16. White Cross	West side of Scotland Road, nearly opposite junction with Bostock Street (OS:SJ34819227).	This marked the northern limit of the Breckshoots section of the Townfield. Its first reference is circa 1300 (42) and it was often referred to as a landmark. Other names for it were the Great Cross and Allan's Cross (43). Besides being referred to obliquely as one of the two Crosses, this White Cross is also named as a landmark in 1508 and 1524 (44).
17. The High Cross	Junction of Castle Street, Dale Street, High Street and Water Street (OS:SJ34219047).	This cross is referred to in 1502 as 'the Cross' (45).
18. Red Cross	Corner of Derby Square and Red Cross Street (OS:SJ34289020).	This cross is marked on a map of 1539 (46).

Sanctuary Stones

Name	Location	Description
19. Castle Street	In the roadway of Castle Street near to the present Town Hall, some 45 metres south of Water Street (OS:SJ34219042).	It marked the limit of the Fair which was first mentioned in 1292. A greenish stone of the Borrowdale Volcanic Series, very probably a glacial erratic, is identified with it; the stone is about 45cm in diameter with four parallel lines scored across it (47).
20. Dale Street	In the roadway, opposite the top of Stanley Street (OS:SJ34399059).	There is no record of its description (48).

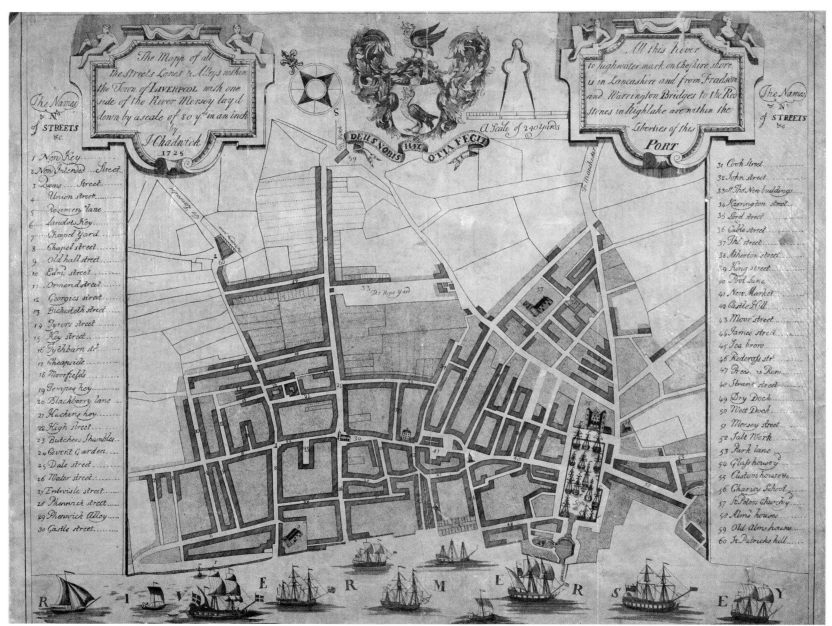

Figure 22: *John Chadwick's 1725 plan of Liverpool is the earliest accurate survey of the town.*

Tudor, Early Stuart and Commonwealth: 1540-1659

Liverpool Town Books, which survive from 1550, are an invaluable source of information about the town and its daily life. Agriculture, and processing agricultural products (meat, vegetables, wool, leather and timber) continued to be the main occupations, along with maritime trade (1). Quarrying for building stone became common. It occurred from at least 1572 on St James's Mount, the site of the Anglican Cathedral, while illicit quarrying took place in Castle Hey, the modern Lord Street/Harrington Street area, in 1587, and on the Heath, a general name for the area across the Pool, in the late 16th century (2). From 1627, quarrying is recorded from Brownlow Hill, the area of the present Liverpool University and the Roman Catholic Cathedral (3).

A court, the Portmoot, was held regularly to enforce bylaws and to order the punishment of law-breakers. Local officials were sworn in at the Portmoot to oversee street cleaning, public health, market and trading activities, managing the Townfield and keeping the Pool clear of rubbish and ballast (4). Every seven years the boundaries of the township with Kirkdale, Everton, West Derby and Toxteth Park townships had to be walked, in order to ensure not only that the Corporation and burgesses knew them, but also that no encroachments were being made (5).

Within the town itself, no noticeable growth took place, and the original seven streets appear in taxation lists. Pool House was built by the Moores in 1557-8 as the first poor house; it later became a house of correction. A further water mill and windmill were built by the end of the sixteenth century. The first salthouse, associated with the production of salt in Cheshire, was in existence by 1636.

One bridge over the Pool existed before 1564, and a new one was added shortly after 1635; their existence may have contributed to the silting up of the Pool. A number of draw wells in the town are referred to but only the Fall Well, across the Pool, can be located (6). The High Cross and White Cross in the town indicated the market areas, while the Townsend and St Patrick's Crosses were erected in addition to the existing wayside crosses.

Butts for archery practice existed at the castle in 1593 (7). There was a gaol beneath the Town Hall, and stocks at the High Cross, but the site of the pillory referred to in 1594 has not been precisely located (8). The ducking stool mentioned in 1578 was known to be at the Flashes near St Patrick's Cross in 1657 (9).

The greatest change to the town's appearance was caused by the erection of fortifications during the Civil War. The Parliamentarians occupied Liverpool in May 1643 and constructed 'mudwalls' (10) while Prince Rupert is reputed to have dug trenches on the Heath when he attacked the town in 1644. The line of the Parliamentarian ramparts and the proposed, but never constructed, Royalist ramparts and defences are shown on a plan made by De Gomme in June 1644 after the Royalist recapture of the town (11). Various trenches and objects of seventeenth century date were uncovered by

work in the present London Road, Copperas Hill and St George's Hall area in the mid eighteenth century and early nineteenth century (12). The 1976 excavations in South Castle Street found the lower part of a ditch system, which might have been of Civil War date (13).

After the Parliamentary recapture of Liverpool, on 1st November 1644, the gates at the end of Tithebarn Street and Chapel Street were taken down (14). Wood for the rebuilding of houses and money to assist in reconstruction were awarded in 1645 and 1648 (15).

On the river a mole or pier was constructed sometime before 1566 (16). Trade with Ireland and Scotland flourished throughout this period. In 1648 the first trading voyage to the Americas took place (17).

The population in the late sixteenth and earlier seventeenth centuries appears to have remained stable. It is estimated at between 100 to 200 households (400 to 1000 people), depending on whether the estimate is based on church or taxation records (18).

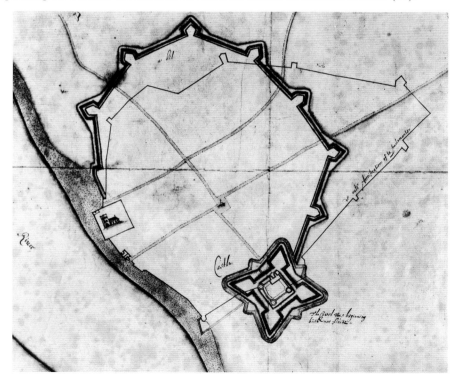

Figure 23:*Civil War plan by de Gomme to make improvements to the town's defences. It shows the original seven streets, The High Cross, Liverpool Castle, St Nicholas' Chapel and The Tower in 1644, after Prince Rupert had seized the town.*

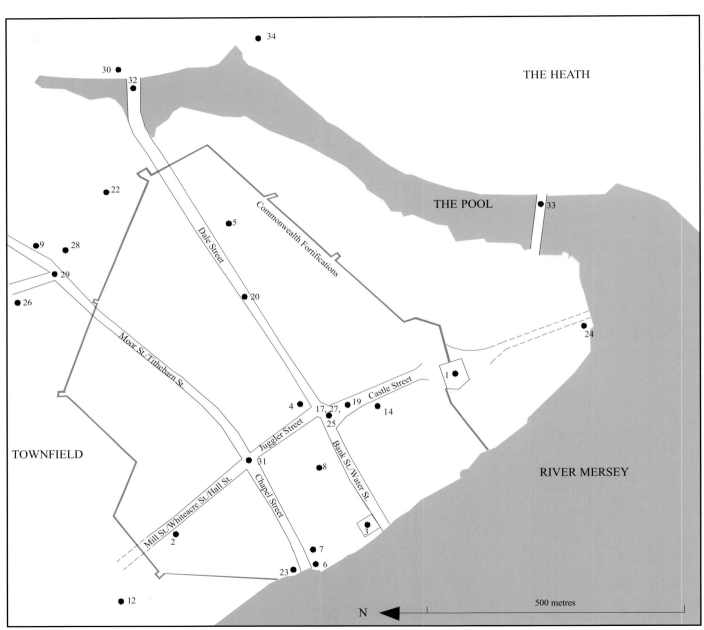

Key:
1. Castle
2. Old (Moore) Hall
3. Tower
4. Town Hall
5. Crosse Hall

Places of Worship
6. St Mary del Key Chapel
7. St Nicholas' Chapel

Commerce and Industry
8. Granary
9. Tithe barn
12. Horse Mill (1)
14. Horse Mill (2)
22. Middle Mill
23. Salt House

Charitable Institutions
24. Pool House

Law and Order
25. Stocks
26. Pinfold
27. Pillory
28. Ducking Stool

Crosses
Wayside Crosses
29. St. Patrick's Cross
30. Townsend Cross
Town Crosses
17. High Cross
31. White Cross

Sanctuary Stones
19. Castle Street
20. Dale Street

Bridges and Wells
32. Townsend Bridge
33. Pool Bridge
34. Fall Well

The following entries in the gazetteer are not shown on the plan:
10, 11, 13, 21, 15, 16, 18

THE HEATH

THE POOL

RIVER MERSEY

TOWNFIELD

Commonwealth Fortifications

Dale Street

Moor St./Tithebarn St.

Castle Street

Juggler Street

Bank St./Water St.

Mill St./Whiteacre St./Hall St.

Chapel Street

500 metres

N

Figure 24: *Tudor, Early Stuart and Commonwealth Plan of Liverpool 1540-1659.*

Name	Location	Description
1. Castle	Derby Square (OS:SJ34269027).	In October 1559 a Royal Commission reported that the Castle was in a poor state; the walls needed repair and the three round towers and the gatehouse tower had no proper roofs left. The report recommended that the great (south west) tower be re-roofed with slate and given new lead gutters. The West Derby Wapentake Court could then be held there and its records safely preserved. The Castle was not needed to defend the harbour, but could act as the stronghold for the town (1). De Gomme's plan of 1644 gives a good contemporary plan. Some repairs to the Castle were made in 1648 (2). In 1659 Parliament was to be petitioned for the Castle walls to be demolished and the ditch filled in (3), but details of what was actually done have not been recorded.
2. Old (Moore) Hall	Under Old Hall Street and Liverpool Echo Building (OS:SJ33999072).	John Moore's widow, Anne, lived at Old Hall from 1575-89 (4). Her will and inventory indicate a relatively modest household and farm as befitted the dower house. The main living quarters were the parlour, hall and great chamber. There were two barns, a shippon, stable and brewhouse in addition to the kitchen, buttery, larder and milkhouse (5).
3. Tower	North side of lower end of Water Street (OS:SJ34009038).	In 1540 the Earl of Derby's stone house (the Tower) was noted by Leland on his tour around England. The Tower was not listed with the Earl's chief houses in 1590 (6). It is shown on De Gomme's plan of 1644. The 7th Lord Derby's estates, including the Tower, were forfeited in 1649 because of his treason to the Commonwealth. The Tower was then used as a temporary prison. After Lord Derby's execution in 1651, it was offered for sale and Alexander Greene, who worked in the prison, contracted to buy it in 1653 (7).
4. Town Hall	East side of High Street near junction with Dale Street (OS:SJ34219050).	There are numerous references to it throughout the period (8).
5. Crosse Hall	Site of Municipal Buildings, south side of Dale Street (OS:SJ34589067).	In 1572 John Crosse applied to build a stone wall to protect his land from the tidal estuary of the Pool (9).

Places of Worship

Name	Location	Description
6. St Mary del Key Chapel	South side of lower end of Chapel Street (OS:SJ33939048).	In 1548 the chapel ceased to be used as such and its endowments were listed (10). It was seized by the King's Commissioners in 1553 and sold to the Corporation for 20 shillings. The building was leased for that same amount yearly and was used first as a school and, from 1572 to 1586 at least, as a storehouse, being described as a little stone house (11). By 1611 it housed the free grammar school of the town (12).

Name	Location	Description
7. St Nicholas' Chapel	South side of lower end of Chapel Street, inland from St Mary del Key (OS:SJ33979047).	When St Mary del Key was closed in 1548, St Nicholas' became the only place of worship in the town. There are numerous references throughout the period to repairs and improvements and levies were imposed to pay for them (13). A clock was installed by 1622 (14), the bells were re-cast in 1636 (15) and a new font provided in 1644 (16). St Nicholas' is shown on De Gomme's plan of 1644.

Commerce and Industry

Name	Location	Description
8. Granary	Near the Water Street end of Rumford Street area (OS:SJ341-904-).	After 1536 the granary was bought by the Moore family (17).
9. Tithe barn	Close to the junction of Marybone and Great CrosshallStreet (OS:SJ344-009-).	The tithe barn is mentioned in records as a landmark, but the building itself was probably used as an ordinary barn from about 1558 (18).
10. Eastham Dale Water Mill	Close to site of John Moores University, Byrom Street campus (OS:SJ348-911-).	See Medieval gazetteer.
11. Eastham Wind Mill	On high ground north west of junction of Gerard Street and Christian Street (OS:SJ349-910-).	Various references to Eastham Windmill imply its continuous usage up to 2 June 1644 when the Royalists captured Liverpool (19). It was destroyed at some point between 1644 and 1646. Plans in 1654 for rebuilding it were never carried out. The usual tenants were the Crosse family, but in 1635 the chief lease was acquired by Lord Molyneux (20).
12. Horse Mill (1)	North west of Old (Moore) Hall in an area west of Old Hall Street and north of Union Street (OS:SJ338-907-).	By 1587, it was no longer used or had been demolished (21). The name Mill Street was still used for most of this period (22), but it had been re-named Hall Street by 1629 (23).
13. Townsend Mill	On the site of the Steble fountain in front of the Walker Art Gallery (OS:SJ35009074).	The mill seems to have operated continuously throughout the period, the Moores usually being the tenants. There are several references to it as a landmark. Like Eastham Windmill the chief lease was acquired by Lord Molyneux in 1635 (24).
14. Horse Mill (2)	Near south corner of junction of Brunswick Street and Castle Street (OS:SJ34229036).	This seems to have continued in use throughout the period.
21. Water Mill	In the area between Stafford Street and Audley Street close to London Road (OS:SJ357-907-).	This watermill belonged to the Norrises and was built before 1587 when it is recorded as operating illegally. It was situated upstream from the site of the former watermill at Eastham Dale and stood below a dam on the stream which flowed from the Moss Lake.

Name	Location	Description
22. Middle Mill	On high ground north of Dale Street, between Johnson Street and North Street (OS:SJ34569086).	This private windmill of the Crosse family was described as ancient in 1587 and was clearly distinguished from the Eastham and Townsend windmills which were royal property (25). In 1641 it was included in a Crosse rental (26).
23. Salt House	North side of Chapel Street, at junction with New Quay (OS:SJ33929053).	This belonged to the Moores and was in existence since at least 1636 (27). It might have been used as one end of the Parliamentary fortifications, for Sir Edward Moore says the old building was fitted with a battery during the civil war, hence its name "Mardyke Fort" (28).
Charitable Institutions 24. Pool House	Under the Queen Elizabeth II Law Courts (OS:SJ343-900-).	Begun in 1557-8 as a Poor House, it was leased by the Moores to the Corporation and used as a house of correction for the poor in 1598 (29) and perhaps as the house of the ferryman (30).
Law and Order 25. Stocks	In front of the present Town Hall (OS:SJ34219047).	Although from 1405 towns were required to maintain stocks, the first surviving record of them at Liverpool is from 1560 (31).
26. Pinfold	Close to junction of Cockspur Street and Vauxhall Road (OS:SJ34389097).	From 1565 there are many references to stray animals being impounded, but there is no description of the structure itself (32). In 1645 a new one was ordered to be made (33).
27. Pillory	In front of the present Town Hall (OS:SJ34219047).	The pillory is assumed to have been next to the stocks. A new pillory was made in 1574 and cost 5s 8d (34).
28. Ducking Stool	South east of the junction of Great Crosshall Street and Hatton Garden (OS:SJ344-908-).	'The Flashes' or 'Watering Place' to the south east of St Patrick's Cross was the location for this form of punishment. Repairs to the ducking stool were ordered in 1578, and a new one was needed in 1637 and in 1657 (35).
Crosses *Wayside Crosses* 15. Everston Cross	West side of Bevington Hill above north slip road from Kingsway Tunnel to Scotland Road (OS:SJ347-917-).	See Medieval gazetteer.
16. White Cross	West side of Scotland Road, nearly opposite junction with Bostock Street (OS:SJ34819227).	See Medieval gazetteer.
29. St. Patrick's Cross	Junction of Hatton Garden, Marybone, Tithebarn Street and Vauxhall Road (OS:SJ34429092).	The references to this cross begin in 1559 (36). It was at the junction of the roads to Kirkdale, Everton and Walton and was beyond the built-up area of the town.
30. Townsend Cross	Close to the junction of WilliamBrown Street and Byrom Street (OS:SJ34789078).	1575 is the first date when this cross is mentioned (37). It stood close to the head of the Pool and near the Townsend Bridge and the road to Prescot. It is noted as a landmark in 1635 (38).

Name	Location	Description
Town Crosses		
17. The High Cross	Junction of Castle Street, Dale Street, High Street and Water Street (OS:SJ34219047).	The name 'High Cross' is mentioned in 1549 perhaps to distinguish it from the White Cross in the town (39). There are many references to proclamations being made at the High Cross and to the market held about it and on its steps (40). It is shown on De Gomme's plan of 1644. In 1653 a candle lantern was ordered to be placed at the High Cross at night time from November to February (41).
18 Red Cross	Corner of Derby Square and Red Cross Street. (OS:SJ34289020).	See Medieval gazetteer.
31. White Cross	Junction of Chapel Street, High Street, Old Hall Street and Tithebarn Street (OS:SJ34129059).	The White Cross in the town is first referred to by name in 1559 (42). There are various notes of it as a landmark and as a centre for part of the market. It was the other place for a candle lantern to be placed at night time from November to February from 1653 (43).
Sanctuary Stones		
19. Castle Street	In the roadway of Castle Street near to the present Town Hall, some 45 metres south of Water Street (OS:SJ34219042).	See Medieval gazetteer. The base of the stone still survives.
20. Dale Street	In the roadway, opposite the top of Stanley Street (OS:SJ34399059).	See Medieval gazetteer.
Bridges and Wells		
32. Townsend Bridge	From the east end of Dale Street across to the west end of William Brown Street (OS:SJ34759076).	The first note of this stone bridge was in 1564 when its repair was ordered. Further repairs were ordered later, and the watercourse had to be cleaned. It stood at the head of the tidal Pool, and streams from the Moss Lake and parts of Everton and Kirkdale flowed into the Pool under it (44).
33. Pool Bridge	Crossing the line of Paradise Street near the junction with College Lane (OS:SJ34559011).	The building of a bridge "where the Sluices were" was ordered in 1635, but the construction was deferred. By 1648 it had been built and was in need of repair in 1655 (45).
34. Fall Well	Queen Square/St John's Lane, close to junction with Roe Street (OS:SJ34869057).	First mentioned in 1568, the Fall Well was a source of fresh water across the Pool. Townspeople were forbidden to clean or wash fleeces, skins and woollen yarn in or near there, but this order was often disobeyed (46).

Figure 25: *The Customs House in 1773 at the head of the Old Dock with the spire of St Thomas' church in the background.*

Figure 26: *The Fall Well and its industrial landscape.*

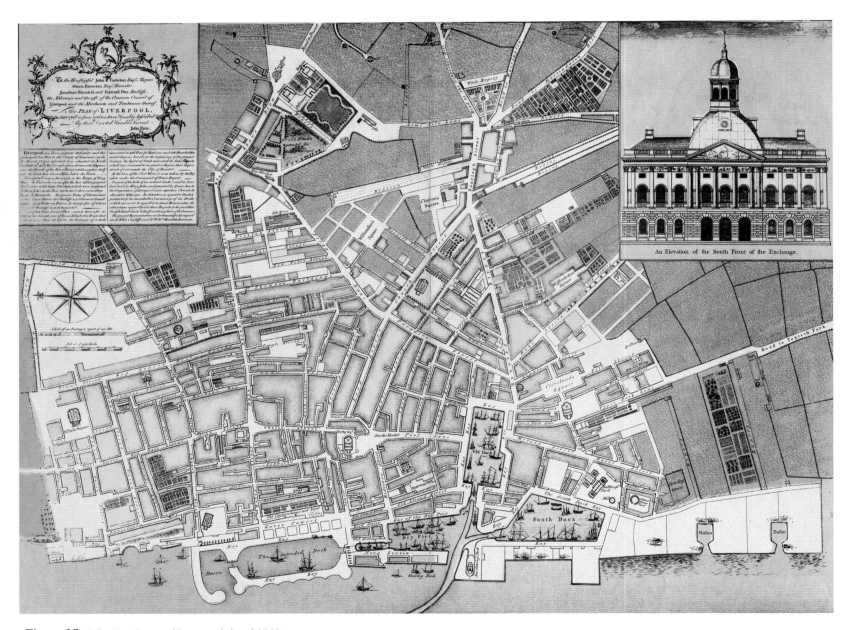

Figure 27: *John Eyes' map of Liverpool dated 1765.*

Later Stuart: 1660-1713

The town began to expand in the late seventeenth and early eighteenth centuries. The 1663 Hearth Tax included just the seven original streets, of which Hall Street had become Old Hall Street by 1663 (1). Juggler Street was first called High Street in 1702, though the old name persisted until about 1710 (2). In the old town area, various land owners laid out additional streets, which are listed in the Moore Rental of 1668 (3) and the Rate Assessment Books of 1705 (which is incomplete) and 1708 (4). Sir Edward Moore laid out several new streets, including Moor Street in 1665 (5) and Bridge Alley, Fenwick Alley and Fenwick Street by 1668; Moorfields was cut through Moore's land after 1668 (6). Lord Molyneux had Lord Street made in 1668 (7). St James's Street was made through Tarleton's field circa 1676, and Red Cross Street through the same field a year later, though until 1705 it was called Tarleton's New Street (8). The large numbers of house-bricks required were made of clay from the Townfield (9) and the sandstone 'slates' were dug from the local quarries.

A new Town Hall and a new Custom House were distinctive features of the expanding town. A new church, St Peter's, was built in 1704 after Liverpool became a parish. As a result of the Indulgence of 1687 and the Toleration Act of 1689, Dissenting Meeting Houses were established. Charitable bequests paid for almshouses to be built and a charity school was opened.

Lord Molyneux erected a bridge across the Pool from the end of Lord Street in 1671 (10). The Lord Street bridge opened up a fresh area beyond the Pool and by 1705 a number of houses and business premises had been built "About ye New Church" of St Peter, including a salt works, dye house and rope works (11).

The Pool continued in existence until the eighteenth century, but it is clear from Corporation records that reclamation was in progress (12). The building of the first almshouses in 1684, close to what had been the head of the Pool, is a clear indication that drainage work had been going on. In 1665 the Corporation built a new quay, whose exact location is unknown (12).

The growth in size of the town can be linked with Liverpool's expanding trade. It ceased to be counted as part of the Port of Chester by 1699, and by 1702 it claimed to be the third busiest trading port in England, the ships sailing mainly to Ireland, Scotland, Europe, North America and the West Indies (13). A major development was the construction of the Wet dock, the first artificial one in the world and the first one in Liverpool, at the mouth of the Pool. The matter was discussed by the Corporation in 1708 and the Act of Parliament passed in 1710. Construction of the dock and reclamation of the upper Pool continued after 1714 (14).

While agriculture and its dependent trades continued to play a major part in the lives of Liverpool's inhabitants, those engaged in maritime trade, in ship-building and its associated crafts, increased every year after 1675 (15). A new industry was refining sugar from the West Indies, the first 'sugar house' being built at the top of Tarleton's field by

1673 (16). Sugar-refining pottery was excavated at South Castle Street (17).

There was a pottery industry on a limited scale (18). The earliest known pot house was located in Lord Street in 1714, though Nicholas Blundell of Little Crosby had seen Delft pottery being made in Liverpool in 1710 (19). Two clay pipe manufacturers lived and worked in Moorfields (20). A direct link between clay pipe manufacture and the import of tobacco from North America from the seventeenth century onwards has been suggested (21). Clay pipes with Liverpool marks are the second-most commonly recovered products (after Glasgow pipes) in North and South America and West Africa (22).

In 1677 the Corporation obtained from Lord Molyneux a lease of the royal milling rights. In 1689 they granted the first of a series of leases permitting the construction of new mills (23). Brick, tile and lime works and the quarries continued in use; 60,000 bricks for the first almshouses were to be made on the Common (24).

The Market remained in the High Street area for much of the period, but by 1714 some produce was sold near the Castle (25). The ducking-stool remained at the Flashes, while the stocks, pillory and cage (lock-up) occupied two sites successively. Some archery butts were located on the Heath near the Townsend bridge.

From the middle of the seventeenth century it is thought that the population expanded rapidly. The Hearth Tax of 1663 suggests a population of between 1300 and 1500. In 1700 the population was around 5000, which rose to around 11,000 in 1730 (26).

Figure 28: *Liverpool in 1728 showing the Old Dock and the wooden jetty which survived until 1744.*

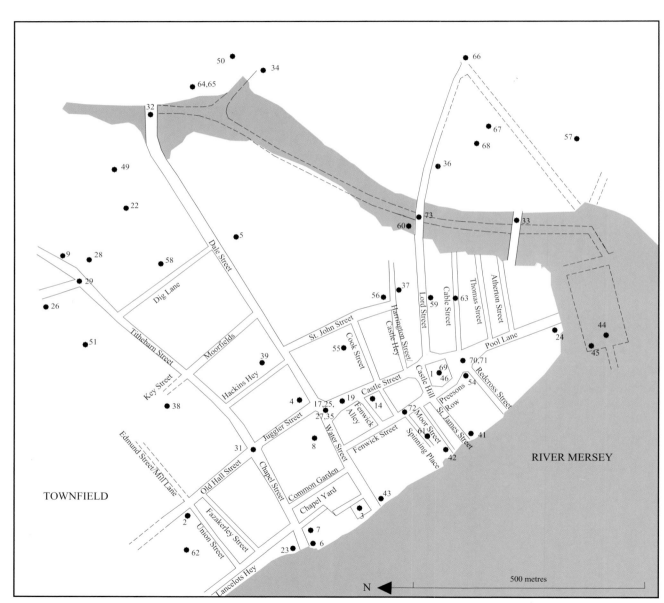

Key:
1. Castle
2. Old Hall
3. Tower
4. First Town Hall
5. Crosse Hall
35. Second Town Hall

Places of worship
6. St Mary del Key
7. St Nicholas' Chapel/Church
36. St Peter's Church
37. Castle Hey Presbyterian Chapel
38. Key Street Presbyterian Chapel
39. Friends' Meeting House
41. Baptist Meeting House

Commerce and Industry
8. Granary
9. Tithe Barn
42. First Custom House
43. Second Custom House
44. Dock: Wet
45. Dock: Dry (Small Graving Dock)
14. Horse Mill (2)
22. Middle Mill (1)
46. Horse Mill (3)
49. Middle Mill (2)
50. Oil Mill
51. Paul's Mill

Other industries
23. Salt House
54. Sugar House
55. Sugar House
56. Sugar House
57. Dye Works
58. Tannery
59. Tannery
60. Pot Works
61. Old Ropery Rope Works
62. Rope Works, Ladies Walk North
63. Rope Works

Charitable Institutions
24. Pool House

Almshouses
64. Poole's Almshouses
65. Richmond's Almshouses
66. Warbrick's Almshouses
67. Charity School
68. Bluecoat School

Law & Order
25. First Stocks
26. Pinfold
27. First Pillory
28. Ducking Stool
69. Second Stocks
70. Second Pillory
71. Cage

Crosses
Wayside
29. St Patrick's Cross
Town
17. High Cross
31. White Cross

Sanctuary Stones
19. Castle Street

Bridges and Wells
32. Townsend Bridge
33. Pool Bridge
72. Dry Bridge
73. Lord Street Bridge
34. Fall Well

The following entries in the gazetteer are not shown on the plan:
40, 10, 11, 12, 13, 21, 47, 48, 52, 53, 15, 16, 18, 20, 30

Figure 29: *Later Stuart Plan of Liverpool 1660-1713.*

Name	Location	Description
1. Castle	Derby Square (OS:SJ34269027).	The 1680 view shows the Castle still to be a substantial building though perhaps not complete. It remained Crown property, controlled by a constable. In 1699, the Corporation started negotiating to acquire the Castle site for a new Church but they obtained only an annual lease in 1700 and full rights over the site were not granted until 1718 (1). In 1704-5, in connection with the lease, two surveys and reports were made, referring to " the remaining ruins" (2). In 1708 it was rated at 10s 0d and the Corporation owned houses built on the outside edge of the moat (3). The south moat seems to have been filled up by 1710 (4). In 1709 permission was granted for a new market to be set up in the Castle area (5). Nicholas Blundell recorded on 31 May 1709 that he went to the Castle to see what alterations had been made (6). On 23 June 1712 he saw the play 'The Yeoman of Kent' performed there and on 13 Oct. 1714 '. . . went to the New-Market where saw a Play acted called Mackbeth.' (7).
2. Old Hall	Under Old Hall Street and Liverpool Echo Building (OS:SJ33999072).	In 1688 the house is described in a survey as '. . . a stone house consisting of six bays in repair, and one little bay of outhousing out of repair . . .': it had a garden and nearly six acres of land (8). When Sir Edward Moore died his son, Cleave Moore, inherited. The Hall was not inhabited in 1708 and, because of his financial difficulties, Sir Cleave Moore retired to the south of England in 1712 (9).
3. Tower	North side of lower end of Water Street (OS:SJ34009038).	Alexander Greene was still the occupant of the Tower in 1663 as he paid tax for nine hearths there but by 1665 the 8th Lord Derby had recovered the estates and the Tower (10). In that year the Tower was leased to Thomas Clayton, a Liverpool merchant, who still held it in 1708 (11). Richard Blome's 'Britannia' of 1673, probably actually published in 1674, included in some copies an expanded section on Liverpool, thought to have been supplied by Sir Edward Moore. He described the Tower as 'a stately and strong pile of buildings' (12). However, in October 1675 it was ordered that the battlements of the Tower be repaired (13). It is shown on the 1680 view.
4. First Town Hall	East side of High Street, near junction with Dale Street (OS:SJ34219050).	The building was still in full use until 1674 when it was ordered that a new Town Hall and Exchange be built at the High Cross. On 22 September 1675, Peter Atherton leased the old building, but the town was to continue to use the storehouse underneath until a new one was built (14). Repairs to the dungeon door were ordered in January 1678. By 1689 the old Common Hall had been converted into two dwelling houses (15).

Name	Location	Description
5. Crosse Hall	Site of Municipal Buildings, south side of Dale Street (OS:SJ3458906-).	The Hall remained in the possession of the Crosse family and is described in Blome as "an ancient manor-house" (16). The Hall and part of the Liverpool estate were leased to Thomas Henshaw in 1697 (17).
35. Second Town Hall	In front of the present Town Hall (OS:SJ34199047).	Blome in 1673 wrote 'Here is now erecting ... a famous town house, placed on pillars and arches of hewn stone, and underneath is the publick exchange of the merchants.' In 1679 it was ordered that a guard house with a room over it be built at the south side (18). The top of the new Town Hall is visible in the 1680 view.

Places of worship

Name	Location	Description
6. St Mary del Key	South side of lower end of Chapel Street (OS:SJ33939048).	Blome notes '. . . a great piece of antiquity, formerly a chappel, now a free school, at the West end whereof, next the river, stood the statue of St Nicholas (long since defaced and gone) to whom the mariners offered when they went to sea . . .' (19). It seems to have been part of the building shown in front of St Nicholas' on the 1680 view.
7. St Nicholas' Chapel/Church	South side of the lower end of Chapel Street, inland from St Mary del Key (OS:SJ33979047).	St Nicholas' was designated a church when Liverpool was made a parish in 1699 and there is constant reference to it in the Vestry Books which survive from 1681. An out-aisle was built on the north side in 1697 (20). It is shown clearly on the 1680 view.
36. St Peter's Church	South side of Church Street opposite Tarleton Street (OS:SJ34649025).	Once Liverpool was designated a parish, this site across the Pool was chosen for a new Church, as the Castle site was not yet available. The building was consecrated on 29 June, 1704. It was a copy of Wren's church of St Andrew in Holborn, London, and cost £3,000 to erect (21).
37. Castle Hey Presbyterian Chapel	South side of Harrington Street, near junction with North John Street (OS:SJ34429033).	In 1692 permission was granted to use Mr David Poole's house in Lord Street for non-conformist worship (22). Mr Poole was listed in the Rate Assessments for 1705 and 1708, in the latter year specifically for a chapel. The actual place of worship was situated in Castle Hey (later called Harrington Street), behind Lord Street. It is not clear if a purpose-built chapel was erected there at some stage, to provide better accommodation (23).
38. Key Street Presbyterian Chapel	Site of Mercury Court complex on north side of Tithebarn Street opposite Moorfields (OS:SJ34209074).	The chapel was built in 1707 as the first building to be erected in Key Street. No rates were charged on it in the 1708 Assessment (24).

Name	Location	Description
39. Friends' Meeting House	Between Leather Lane and Hackins Hey (OS:SJ34259059).	The Meeting House, bought in 1711, had a burying-ground beneath. The building is mentioned in the Rate Assessment of 1708 as being owned by Mr Thomas Preeson (25).
40. Roman Catholic Places of Worship	North John Street.	Between 1707 and 1715 two houses in St John Street (now North John Street) were used successively for Roman Catholic worship; they cannot be located precisely (26).
41. Baptist Meeting House	At the Strand Street end of James Street (OS:SJ341-902-).	In 1710 the Town Book records that Dr Daniel Fabius' house was a meeting place for Protestant dissenters. In 1700 he had been given similar permission for his house in Everton (27).

Commerce and Industry

Name	Location	Description
8. Granary	Near the Water Street end of Rumford Street (OS:SJ341-904-).	In 1668 Sir Edward Moore identified the building as the former Birkenhead Priory granary. Moore's tenant, Jonathan Hunter, virtually reconstructed the place, taking down the outside steps and re-using the stones. Moore wrote that a neighbour in Water Street had recently built a wall with a door in it, effectively closing in the former granary from the street and impeding access to it (28).
9. Tithe barn	Close to the junction of Marybone and Great Crosshall Street (OS:SJ344-009-).	The barn seems to have been demolished before 1674 since, in that year, a survey was to be carried out of the Flashes (the pool on the south side of St Patrick's Cross) and the land close to it, near the place where the old Tithe barn had stood (29). This locates the barn beyond the Flashes, and not on the town side (30). There are two barns listed in Tithebarn Street in the 1708 Rate Assessment and one of them later appears to have been mistaken for the (destroyed) Tithe barn (31).
42. First Custom House	On the north side of Moor Street, at the junction with The Strand (OS:SJ341902-).	At first the Custom House was situated in the Town Hall (32). When the new Town Hall was built in 1673-74 the Custom House was located for a short time in a house in the newly-cut Moor Street (33).
43. Second Custom House	At the south corner of The Strand and Water Street (OS:SJ34029036).	In 1680 Sylvester Moorcroft leased out his new building on the water front. It is shown on the 1680 view and in 1708 was rated at £1 2s 4d (34). The building appears to have been of stone, of at least two storeys and with several chimney stacks.
44. Dock: Wet	Canning Place (OS:SJ34388996).	The first Dock Act was passed in 1709 and Thomas Steers was instructed to proceed with the works in 1710 (35). On 22nd July 1710 Nicholas Blundell recorded going to see the dock being made (36). In 1980 and 2001 excavations revealed the First Dock wall (37).

Name	Location	Description
45. Dock: Dry (Small Graving Dock)	Canning Dock (OS:SJ23238996).	A small graving dock was constructed by Alderman Norris and his partners on a site to the north of the entrance to the wet dock, leased from the Corporation. Some of the stone came from the Brownlow Hill quarry (38).
10. Eastham Dale Water Mill	Close to site of John Moores University, Byrom Street campus (OS:SJ348-911-).	See Medieval gazetteer.
11. Eastham Wind Mill	On high ground north west of junction of Gerard Crescent and Christian Street (OS:SJ349-910-).	See Tudor, Early Stuart and Commonwealth gazetteer.
12.Horse Mill (1)	North West of Old (Moore) Hall in an area west of Old Hall Street and north of Union Street (OS:SJ338-907-).	See Medieval and Tudor, Early Stuart and Commonwealth gazetteers.
13. Townsend Mill	On the site of the Steble fountain in front of the Walker Art Gallery (OS:SJ35009074).	The Moores were once again tenants of the mill, although in 1668 it was mortgaged (39). Sunday grinding there was fined in 1672 (40). The Rate Assessments for 1705 and 1708 note Sir Cleave Moore as tenant for the mill (41).
14. Horse Mill (2)	Near south corner of junction of Brunswick Street and Castle Street (OS:SJ34229036).	Sir Edward Moore in 1668 wrote at length about milling in general and about this mill in particular, as the income derived from it was considerable (42). It is mentioned in the 1705 Rate Assessment as being the property of Sir Cleave Moore, but in 1708 it was leased to a William Rawlins (43). There are no references to it after this period. The mill gave rise to the name of an inn called the Millstone which stood near it on the east side of Castle Street. The Millstone was the starting point for one of the two stagecoach services from Liverpool in 1766.
21. Water Mill	In the area between Stafford Street and Audley Street, close to London Road (OS:SJ357-907-).	The mill is listed in the 1708 Rate Assessment and noted as a landmark (44).
22. Middle Mill (1)	On high ground north of Dale Street between Johnson Street and North Street (OS:SJ34569086).	The mill is referred to in Moore's rental of 1668 as Mr. Crosse's windmill (45). In 1672 there were fines for grinding corn there on Sundays (46). According to the Rate Assessments for 1705 and 1708, it was being leased by William Shaw (47).
46. Horse Mill (3)	In Derby Square (OS:SJ34269027).	A horse mill in the Castle is referred to between 1663 and 1668 (48).
47. Horse Mill (4)	Castle Street.	A horse mill here is referred to in 1705 and 1708, but its precise location is not given nor is it mentioned after this period (49).

Later Stuart Gazetteer

Name	Location	Description
48. Horse Mill (5)	High Street.	A mill, likely to have been a horse-mill, is mentioned in the 1708 Rate Assessment but its exact position is not noted, and it is not mentioned after this period (50).
49. Middle Mill (2)	North of Dale Street, on the west side of Trueman Street (OS:SJ34619084).	This may be the 'newer Miln' of Richard Norris, referred to in the Rate Assessment of 1705 in the list of Wind Mills. In 1708 a Mr. William Gee leased a house and mill listed under Dale Street, but it is not referred to as Norris's mill then or subsequently (51).
50. Oil Mill	On the site of St George's Hall (OS:SJ349-906-).	Oil was produced by crushing the rape plant's oil-bearing seeds. The mill was mentioned in the 1705 and 1708 Rate Assessments, but in the former it was referred to as a landmark only, not listed under windmills, so it may have been in the course of construction (52).
51. Paul's Mill	Corner of Smithfield Street and Cockspur Street (OS:SJ34289094).	Paul Culcheth's 'New Miln' is listed in the 1705 and 1708 Rate Assessments and there are several references to it as a landmark. The lane leading to it from Old Hall Street was called Mill Lane, Mill-house Lane or Mill-hill Lane before it was re-named Edmund Street (53).
52. Park Mill	To the west of the junction between Park Lane and Jamaica Street (OS:SJ34758942).	The first note of this mill occurs in the Rate Assessment of 1708 where it is referred to as a landmark (54).
Other industries		
23. Salt House	North side of Chapel Street, at the junction with New Quay (OS:SJ33929053).	This was referred to in 1676 as the old salthouse or store house (55). In 1708 it was rated at 6s and it is mentioned in St Nicholas' Register in 1713 (56).
53. Salt Works	East quay of present Salthouse Dock (OS:SJ34428973).	In 1696 Jonathan and John Blackburne petitioned the Corporation for permission to erect a Salt Works to the South of the Pool (57). It belonged to Mr Blackburn according to the Rate Books of 1705 and 1708 (58).
54. Sugar House	Close to north west corner of junction of Red Cross Street and Derby Square (OS:SJ34259022).	The first sugar refinery was a five-storey building put up by Richard Cleveland and Daniel Danvers between 1670 and 1673. It was rated in both 1705 and 1708 (59).
55. Sugar House	North side of Union Court and west of North John Street (OS:SJ34309044).	Mr John Hughes was rated in 1705 and 1708 for this sugar house (60).
56. Sugar House	North west corner of Harrington Street and North John Street (OS:SJ3440 9035).	In 1705 Mr Daniel Danvers was rated for this sugar house. By 1708 it had passed to "Mr. Jon. Tattlock". It was listed under Lord Street (61).

Name	Location	Description
57. Dye Works	South west of Gilbert Street on the line of Greetham Street(OS:SJ34778975).	The 'dyehouse' is recorded in the 1705 Rate Assessment and was noted as a landmark in 1708 (62). It was situated 'Over the Pool' some distance away from the town.
58. Tannery	On the west side of Hatton Garden behind the Magistrates Courts in Dale Street (OS:SJ34469080).	Mr Thomas Henshaw was rated at 3s 8d in 1708 for a house and tan yard, listed under Dale Street (63).
59. Tannery	Lord Street (OS:SJ34489078).	Richard Mercer had a tan house somewhere in Lord Street in 1708 (64).
60. Pot Works	North west corner of Lord Street and Whitechapel (OS:SJ34549031).	In 1714 Alderman Josiah Poole was granted a lease of property for use as a pot or mug house. He had a tile-works from 1701, listed as 'Over the Pool' in 1708 (65).
61. Old Ropery Rope Works	Old Ropery Street (OS:SJ34149028).	William Bushell had a rope walk on the site at an unknown date.
62. Rope Works, Ladies Walk North	Between Old Hall Street and Bath Street, north of Brook Street (OS:SJ33869084).	The tree-lined (North) Ladies Walk ran between Old Hall Street and the North Shore (66). Its shape suggests it was originally the site of a rope walk. In Oct 1668 John Bamber, Ropemaker, was admitted tenant at will of a "spinning place" in the Old Hall Lane (67).
63. Rope Works	Cable Street, under Grosvenor development (2007) (OS:SJ34369022).	The Town Records of 1701 mention this street as originally a rope making centre (68). This may be the site "near the Park Gate" that Alderman William Clayton petitioned for a "spinning place" in 1692 (69).

Charitable Institutions

24. Pool House	Under the Queen Elizabeth II Law Courts (OS:SJ343-900-).	It is mentioned by Moore in his 1668 Rental in use as a House of Correction (70).

Almshouses

64. Poole's Almshouses	South side of William Brown Street near the foot of St John's Gardens (OS:SJ34829073).	The Town Book entry for 7 May 1684, records that permission was granted for twelve almshouses to be built and it is thought that Mr David Poole paid for them (71). They were the first recorded almshouses.

Name	Location	Description
65. Richmond's Almshouses	South side of William Brown Street, near the foot of St John's Gardens (OS:SJ34829073).	On 12 April 1692, Dr Silvester Richmond gave £100 to build another block of almshouses for poor sailors' widows (72). They were built as an annex to Poole's Houses. Dr Richmond's widow later left £50 to pay for repairs and the Corporation administered the fund (73).
66. Warbrick's Almshouses	At the junction of Bold Street and Hanover Street (OS:SJ34849018).	In his will of 1706 Richard Warbrick, mariner, left £120 for the Corporation to build "one Almshouse with eight roomes.. ' for poor sailors' widows'". In 1708 the Corporation undertook to keep them in repair in consideration of an extra £30 paid by Warbrick's executors (74).
67. Charity School	South side of School Lane, east of the Blue Coat Chambers (OS:SJ34739016).	In 1708 former sea captain Bryan Blundell bought a small schoolhouse (75).
68. Bluecoat School	School Lane (OS:SJ34689015).	In 1709 Bryan Blundell and Robert Stythe established a charity school for poor boys. The cost of running it for fifty children was met by voluntary subscription (76).

Law & Order

Name	Location	Description
25. First Stocks	In front of the present Town Hall (OS:SJ34219047).	It is presumed that the stocks remained here until the new Town Hall was built in 1673.
26. Pinfold	Close to junction of Cockspur Street and Vauxhall Road (OS:SJ34389097).	It is mentioned as a landmark in the 1708 Rate Assessment (77).
27. First Pillory	In front of the present Town Hall (OS:SJ34219047).	The Town Book for 28 April 1679 recorded that a pillory was to be built in some convenient place in the town (78). This was presumably because the new Town Hall now occupied the old site by the High Cross.
28. Ducking Stool	South east of the junction of Great Crosshall Street and Hatton Garden (OS:SJ344-908-).	Moore refers in 1668 to a woman having been ducked. The stool was repaired in 1695 at a cost of 15s, and in 1712 a new one had to be ordered (79).
69. Second Stocks	Derby Square (OS:SJ34279024).	Nicholas Blundell recorded in his diary that he saw people in the stocks in 1705 (80).
70. Second Pillory	Derby Square (OS:SJ34279024).	Nicholas Blundell recorded that he saw someone standing in the pillory in 1711 (81).
71. Cage	In Derby Square, close to the top of Red Cross Street (OS:SJ34279021).	The Town Book for 28 April, 1679 recorded that a cage (lock-up) was to be built in some convenient place in the town (82).

Name	Location	Description
Crosses		
Wayside Crosses		
15. Everston Cross	West side of Bevington Hill above the slipway from The Kingsway Tunnel to Scotland Road (OS:SJ347-917-).	See Medieval gazetteer.
16. White Cross	West side of Scotland Road, nearly opposite junction with Bostock Street (OS:SJ34819227).	See Medieval gazetteer.
29. St Patrick's Cross	Junction of Hatton Garden, Marybone, Tithebarn Street and Vauxhall Road (OS :SJ34429092).	See Tudor, Early Stuart and Commonwealth gazetteers.
Town Crosses		
17. High Cross	Junction of Castle Street, Dale Street, High Street and Water Street (OS: SJ34219047).	When the new Town Hall was built in 1673-4 the High Cross was taken down. On 25 May, 1674 Thomas Mathews was fined 6s 8d for objecting to its removal (83).
18. Red Cross	Corner of Derby Square and Red Cross Street. (OS:SJ34289020).	See Medieval gazetteer.
30. Townsend Cross	Close to the junction of William Brown Street and Byron Street (OS:SJ34789078).	See Tudor, Early Stuart and Commonwealth gazetteers.
31. White Cross	Junction of Chapel Street, High Street, Old Hall Street and Tithebarn Street (OS: SJ34129059).	A general market was held there after 1673 and it was the chief market for potatoes. It was noted in the Town Book on 28 October 1701 that the tolls of fruit were usually collected at the White Cross. The market was removed to the site of St John's Market in 1822 (84).
Sanctuary Stones		
19. Castle Street	In the roadway of Castle Street near the present Town Hall (OS: SJ34219042).	See Medieval gazetteer.
20. Dale Street	In the roadway, opposite the top of Stanley Street (OS:SJ34399059).	See Medieval gazetteer.
Bridges and Wells		
32. Townsend Bridge	From the east end of Dale Street across to the west end of William Brown Street (OS:SJ34759076).	Further repairs were ordered in 1665 (85), but there seem to be no further references to it, perhaps because drainage and reclamation work were progressing (86).

Name	Location	Description
33. Pool Bridge	Crossing the line of Paradise Street near the junction with College Lane (OS:SJ34559011).	The bridge continued in use and repairs were ordered in 1662 and 1665. The 'battlements' needed in 1679 were for the security of travellers at night (87). Repairs were again necessary in 1685, but there seem to be no further references to it, perhaps because drainage and reclamation work were progressing (88).
72. Dry Bridge	Junction of Fenwick Street and Old Ropery (OS:SJ34199032).	A stone bridge built before 1668 by order of Sir Edward Moore over a dry, rock-cut gully which ran from the area of Lower Castle Street along the line of Old Ropery. The gully may originally have formed part of an outer ditch of the Castle (89).
73. Lord Street Bridge	Across Whitechapel between Lord Street and Church Street (OS:SJ34559029).	The Town Book for 23 March 1670 recorded opposition to Lord Molyneux's plan to build a new bridge across the Pool. The 70 yards (60 metres) of planking which he laid down were removed, but after negotiation in 1671, the bridge was allowed (90). There do not seem to be later references to it, perhaps because drainage and reclamation work took place (91). Remains of stone abutments and part of an arch were uncovered during building excavations in the area in the1850s (92).
34. Fall Well	Queen Square/St John's Lane, close to junction with Roe Street (OS:SJ34869057).	This continued to be a main source of fresh water during the period, though Moore recorded in 1668 that the tenants in the newly-cut Moor Street used an excellent well he had had dug. Repairs to the Fall Well were necessary in 1679 and 1694, and no washing was to be done there (93).

Figure 30: *Plan (in four quadrants) of the Town and Port of Liverpool by George Perry 1769.*

George I - George III: 1714-1770

In the eighteenth century the town of Liverpool continued to grow rapidly. The area between the castle site and the former Pool was further developed. The parts formerly 'over the Pool' became more readily accessible, and more streets were laid out there. Chadwick's map of 1725 was intended to provide a street plan but, although some major buildings are drawn in detail, the Castle, Old Hall, Crosse Hall and the Tower are not even named. John Eyes' plan of 1765 and William Perry's of 1769 show the expansion of the town during the subsequent forty years. It is estimated that by 1756 the town had 222 streets, up from 22 in 1698 (1).

During this period, the first wet dock became fully operational, and two more docks, the Salthouse and the Manchester, were planned and opened. Dry docks and a new Custom House were built. Three new Church of England churches were erected as well as several chapels and meeting places for Protestant dissenters and a Jewish meeting place. There was even a Roman Catholic chapel in a discreet location, as at this time Catholics were not allowed to worship openly.

Two buildings of this period have survived to the present day. One is the Town Hall, which was designed by John Wood of Bath, built in 1748-1754, altered in 1789-92 to designs by James Wyatt and remodelled after a fire in 1795. The other is Bluecoat Chambers, which began as a Charity School founded by Bryan Blundell and was completed in 1726. Both are Grade 1 Listed buildings.

It is evident from the Town Books (2) that agriculture was still important. Enclosures, which had already begun, were made in increasing numbers through the 18th century, though some individual strips remained in the communal Townfield (3). There was a great increase in the digging of clay for bricks and pottery (4).

Salt from Cheshire continued to be brought down the Weaver both for onward transport and for use in food preservation, tanning, glass-making and pottery-making in the town. The canalization of the River Weaver in 1733 allowed greater amounts to be shipped: 20,000 tons a year by 1760 and 100,000 tons per year by the end of the century (5). Manufacturing industries such as ship-building, rope-making, iron-working, clock-making, pottery manufacture, and glass-making thrived during the century (6). In 1765-6 over 50% of occupations listed in a sample of baptismal records were in manufacturing, but the proportion had dropped to fewer than 30% by 1810 (7).

The number of ships belonging to the port was 113 in 1716, rising to 309 in 1770. The number of ships using the port increased from 370 inwards and 409 outwards in 1716, to 806 inwards and 1021 outwards in 1770. The increase of ships trading with Africa was even more marked, up from 1 in 1709 to 96 in 1770 (8). These ships were part of the triangular trade that involved taking manufactured goods to West Africa, picking up cargoes of slaves and carrying them to the West Indies and North America, and bringing back to Liverpool cargoes of sugar, tobacco and cotton. By 1748 Liverpool had outstripped Bristol in the slave trade, and a memorandum of 1752 lists 101 Liverpool

business men participating in the Africa trade (9). Many jobs in the town depended on producing goods for the Africa trade, or processing raw products from the Americas, so that there was much opposition to the idea of abolishing the slave trade. However, due to an increase in other cargoes, the port continued to prosper after the slave trade was banned in 1807.

The population increased rapidly, from 11,932 in 1730 to 18,400 in 1750 and 34,050 in 1770 (10). This is likely to be due greatly to the inward migration of workers from the surrounding areas to a flourishing town with many opportunities for work.

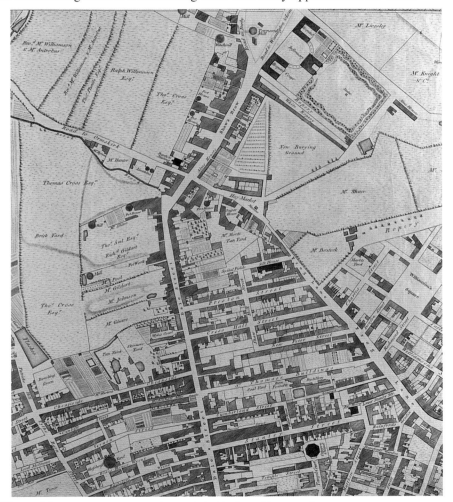

Figure 31: *North east section of Perry's 1769 plan of Liverpool.*

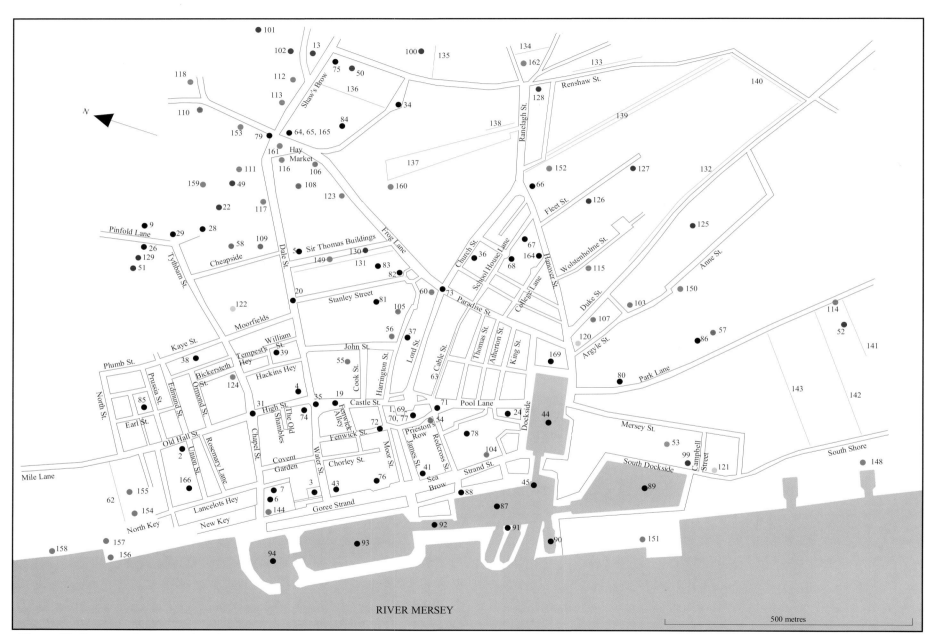

Figure 32: *George I - George III plan of Liverpool 1714-1770.*

George 1- George III: 1714-1770

Municipal and lordship
 1. Castle
 2. Old Hall
 3. Tower
 4. First Town Hall
 5. Crosse Hall
 35. Second Town Hall
 74. Third Town Hall
 75. Infirmary
 76. Playhouse

Places of worship
 6. St Mary del Key
 7. St Nicholas' Church
 36. St Peter's Church
 37. Castle Hey Presbyterian Chapel
 38. Key Street Presbyterian Chapel
 39. Friends' Meeting House
 41. First Baptist Meeting House
 77. St George's Church
 78. Benn's Garden Presbyterian Chapel
 79. Second Baptist Meeting House
 80. St Thomas' Church
 81. Octagon Chapel
 82. Third Baptist Meeting House
 83. Synagogue
 84. New Burying Ground
 85. St Paul's Church
 86. Pitt Street Methodist Chapel

Commerce
 9. Tithe Barn
 43. Second Custom House
 169. Third Custom House

Docks
 44. Dock: Wet
 45. Dry Dock (Small Graving Dock)
 87. Dock: Dry
 88. Slipway
 89. Dock: South
 90. Dock: Dry (Graving Dock)
 91. Dock: Dry (Graving Dock)
 92. Dock: Dry (Graving Dock)
 93. Dock: New (George's Dock)
 94. Dock: New Dry (George's Dock Basin)

Industry
● *Mills*
 13. Townsend Mill
 22. Middle Mill (1)
 49. Middle Mill (2)
 50. Oil Mill
 51. Paul's Mill
 52. Park Mill
 99. Windmill
 100. Windmill
 101. Mill
 102. Windmill
● *Salt*
 53. Saltworks
● *Sugar*
 54. Sugar House
 55. Sugar House
 56. Sugar House
 103. Cleveland Square Sugar House
 104. Sugarhouse Yard
 105. Hughes Sugar House
 106. Sugar House
 107. Sugar House
● *Dying & tanning*
 57. Dye Works
 58. Tannery
 108. Mr Mort's Tanyard
 109. Skinner's Yard
 110. Tanyard
● *Pot Works*
 60. Pot Works
 111. Pot Works
 112. Pot Works
 113. Pot Works
 114. Pot Works
 115. Pot Works
 116. Pot Works
 117. Potworks
 118. Mr Livesley's Mughouse
● *Glass works*
 120. Glass Works
 121. Glass Works
 122. Glass Works
● *Silk*
 123. Silkhouse
 124. Silkhouse
● *Brewing & Distilling*
 125. Brewery
 126. Brewery
 127. Mr. Crosbie's Brewery
 128. Brewery

 129. Brewery
 130. Distillery
Ropewalks
 62. Rope Works: Ladies Walk North
 63. Rope Works
 131. Rope Works
 132. Rope Works: Ladies Walk South
 133. Rope Walk
 134. Rope Works: White Ropery
 135. Rope Works
 136. Rope Works
 137. Rope Works
 138. Rope Works
 139. Rope Walk
 140. Rope Works
 141. Rope Works
 142. Rope Works
 143. Rope Works
● *Other Buildings*
 144. Battery and Magazine
 148. Copper Works
 149. Iron Foundry
 150. Iron Foundry
 151. Iron Foundry
 152. Limekilns
 153. Limekilns
 154. Limekiln
 155. Brickyard
 156. The Baths
 157. Machine
 158. Boatyard
 159. Brickyard
 160. Marble yard
 161. Machine
 162. Ranelagh Pleasure Gardens

Charitable Institutions
 24. Pool House
 164. Workhouse or Poor House
Almshouses
 64. Poole's Almshouses
 65. Richmond's Almshouses
 66. Warbrick's Almshouses
 165. Scarsbrick's Almshouses
Schools
 67. Charity School
 68. The Bluecoat School
 166. Mr Chalmers School

Law & Order
 26. Pinfold
 28. Ducking Stool
 69. Second Stocks
 70. Second Pillory
 71. Cage

Crosses and Sanctuary Stones
Wayside Crosses
 29. St Patrick's Cross
Town Crosses
 31. White Cross
Sanctuary Stones
 19. Castle Street
 20. Dale Street

Bridges and Wells
 72. Dry Bridge
 73. Lord Street Bridge (site of)
 34. Fall Well

The following entries in the gazetteer are not shown on the plan:
40, 8, 42, 10, 12, 14, 46, 47, 48, 95, 96, 97, 98, 23, 59, 119, 61, 145, 146, 147, 163, 25, 27, 15, 16, 17, 18, 30, 32, 33

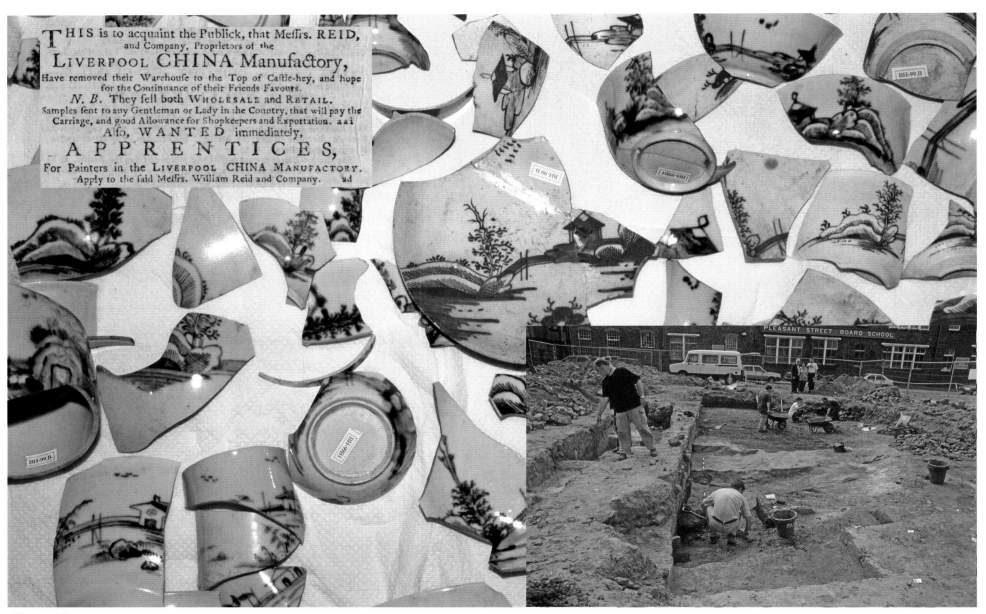

THIS is to acquaint the Publick, that Meſſrs. REID, and Company, Proprietors of the

LIVERPOOL CHINA Manufactory,

Have removed their Warehouſe to the Top of Caſtle-hey, and hope for the Continuance of their Friends Favours.

N. B. They ſell both WHOLESALE and RETAIL.

Samples ſent to any Gentleman or Lady in the Country, that will pay the Carriage, and good Allowance for Shopkeepers and Exportation. aaı

Alſo, WANTED immediately,

APPRENTICES,

For Painters in the LIVERPOOL CHINA MANUFACTORY. Apply to the ſaid Meſſrs. William Reid and Company. ad

Figure 33: *Fragments of porcelain recovered during the excavation at the site of William Reid's china factory in 1997-98. Inset: the excavation in progress and an advertisement by Messrs Reid dated 1759.*

George I-George III Gazetteer

Name	Location	Description
Municipal and lordship		
1. Castle	Derby Square (OS: SJ34269027).	The Corporation lease did not convey full rights over the Castle site until 1718 when the Letters Patent were received. There were still tenants in the round tower until that date and they were then given notice to quit (1). Parts of the Castle seem to have stood in 1725, as shown in the east and west sides of the new market on Chadwick's map. On 1 February 1726 it was ordered that the Castle wall at the top of Lord Street should be pulled down so that a new church could be built (2).
2. Old Hall	Under Old Hall Street and Liverpool Echo Building (OS:SJ33999072).	The Moore estates were sold to Lord Derby in 1724 (3). Perry's 1769 plan shows an L-shaped building. The land had gradually been encroached upon, but the house stood intact until 1820 when a Street Improvement Act meant that part of the Hall had to be taken down. The rest of the house was demolished subsequently (4).
3. Tower	North side of lower end of Water Street (OS:SJ34009038).	The building was used as a prison for some rebels in 1715-16, and some windows were bricked up for greater security (5). Richard Clayton bought the Tower from the Derby family in 1717. The Corporation leased the property in 1737 and, in 1745, conversion of part to a prison was arranged. The upper rooms were used for assemblies and entertainments until the new Town Hall was ready in 1754. The Tower was bought by the Corporation in 1774 and refurbished for continued use as the Borough Gaol. By July 1811 the gaol was closed with the transfer of the remaining prisoners to the new Borough Gaol in Great Howard Street. The Tower itself was demolished in October 1819 in the widening of Water Street (6).
4. First Town Hall	East side of High Street, near junction with Dale Street (OS: SJ3421 9050).	Part of the building continued to be used as a prison. The Town Book entry for it in January 1737 recorded that the prison in High Street was too small, and vaults under the Tower were recommended instead. The John Eyes' plan of 1765 indicated that the site was still Corporation property (7).
5. Crosse Hall	Site of Municipal Buildings, south side of Dale Street (OS:SJ34589067).	The Crosse family retained possession of the Hall. Richard Crosse's will of 1742 bequeathed the Hall to his wife Ann, and others (8). About 1750 the estate was sold and laid out for building, and the Hall was demolished (9).
35. Second Town Hall	In front of the present Town Hall (OS:SJ34199047).	It is shown on the Bucks' view of 1728. The building was in a dangerous state in 1740, the pillars and one of the arches had begun to sink and the turret was to be taken down. The building was demolished in 1755 (10).

George I-George III Gazetteer

Name	Location	Description
74. Third Town Hall	Still extant (OS:SJ34199047).	A new Town Hall was built behind the second one, on the present site, and was opened in 1754. It was damaged by fire in 1795, but restored and extended by 1811 (11).
75. Infirmary	East end of William Brown Street under St.George's Hall (OS:SJ34999069).	A public subscription list to raise funds for a new Liverpool Infirmary was opened 1744. The site chosen for the building was Oyl Mill field and some waste land adjoining it at the top of Shaw's Brow. In July 1745, during work on the foundations, remains of infantry positions constructed by Prince Rupert in 1644 were found. The building was opened on 25th March 1749 with three floors to house 100 patients plus attics and cellars. In April 1752, two plots of land (one each side) were granted to the Seamen's Hospital Trustees for two buildings that would contain a number of almshouses for the use of aged seamen and their families or seamen's widows and orphans, to be supported by a levy from sailors' pay. In 1765 John Tarleton made a gift of a turret clock for the Infirmary. In 1771 the Infirmary was extended by a new west ward and new east wing. In 1824 it transferred to a new site in Brownlow Street and the old building was demolished in 1826. In 1789 the trustees purchased the ropery which bordered the west side of the Infirmary in order to build a lunatic asylum, which was completed in 1792. The new building had a frontage onto St John's Lane and accommodation for 64 patients. It remained in use until a new asylum was opened in 1831 (12).
76. Playhouse	Drury Lane (OS:SJ34129031).	In 1746 Alderman Thomas Steers, the engineer of the Old Dock, had a building erected for dramatic performances in the Old Ropery opposite the end of Drury Lane, next to a cockpit fronting Moor Street (13). Measuring only 50 feet by 20 feet the site proved too small (14) and a new theatre was constructed on the east side of Drury Lane, opening in 1759. It was pulled down in 1788 and part of its site now forms a portion of Brunswick Street. A second theatre, the Theatre Royal, was opened in 1772 on the north side of Williamson Square (15).

George I-George III Gazetteer

Name	Location	Description
Places of worship		
6. St Mary del Key	South side of lower end of Chapel Street (OS:SJ33939048).	The building is shown on Chadwick's 1725 map and on subsequent maps and plans including Horwood's map of 1803. In 1745, the Church Vestry directed that since the school was ruinous, it should be taken down but in 1766 "the late old school in the churchyard" was still being used as the Ince Boat House (16). Herdman later painted a retrospective view of St Nicholas' in 1760 and included the Boat House (17). The Corporation sold the property to the Rectors and Churchwardens of the parish of Liverpool in May 1814 and it was demolished in the same year. The land was subsequently consecrated as an addition to the churchyard of St Nicholas (18).
7. St Nicholas' Church	South side of the lower end of Chapel Street, inland from St Mary del Key (OS:SJ33979047).	An addition to the out-aisle was built in 1718. The Church is shown clearly on the Bucks' view of 1728. Later, in 1746, a spire was built on the old tower. The nave and south aisle were demolished and rebuilt in 1775. The north aisle and its out-aisle were demolished in 1780 and the north aisle reconstructed. The tower and spire collapsed in 1810 and the tower was rebuilt in 1815 (19). This tower remains, but the rest of the church had to be rebuilt, in 1952, as a result of the 1939-45 war. There are details of alterations to the interior of the church, and to the churchyard, in the Vestry Books (20).
36. St Peter's Church	South side of Church Street, opposite Tarleton Street (OS:SJ34649025).	The Church is shown on the Bucks' view of 1728. It had the first Library in Liverpool, founded by a bequest of John Fells, mariner, in 1715. The church was demolished in 1922; a brass cross in the paved area of Church Street marks its site (21).
37. Castle Hey Presbyterian Chapel	South side of Harrington Street, near junction with North John Street (OS: SJ34429033).	The chapel continued in use until 1727 when the congregation moved to a larger chapel built in Benn's Garden (22).
38. Key Street Presbyterian Chapel	Site of Mercury Court complex on north side of Tithebarn Street opposite Moorfields (OS:SJ34209074).	The chapel was used until 1791 when the congregation moved to a new chapel in Paradise Street. The old chapel became St Matthew's Church of England church, and was demolished in 1848 when Exchange Station was being built (23).
39. Friends' Meeting House	Between Leather Lane and Hackins Hey (OS:SJ34259054) .	The Society of Friends continued to use this building until 1791 when they moved to Hunter Street. The old premises were used as a school from 1813 to 1861, when they were sold and demolished (24).

George I-George III Gazetteer

Name	Location	Description
40. Roman Catholic Places of Worship	a) Near to the south west corner of Edmund Street and Old Hall Street (OS:SJ34049072). b) Behind Mercury Court between the ends of Ormond Street and Edmund Street (OS:SJ34139078).	In 1715 Nicholas Blundell began negotiating with Sir Cleave Moore's lawyer for a piece of land. By Easter 1727 the chapel, part of Father John Hardisty's house, was virtually complete and in use. It was destroyed in 1746 in riots following the Jacobite uprising of 1745. A new site was chosen round the corner between Bixteth Street and Lumber Street, close to the west side of the former Exchange Station site. The church was constructed like a warehouse in order to avoid notice, but it was damaged during a riot in 1759. Subsequently repaired, it was enlarged in 1797, and it continued in use until St. Mary's was built on the same site and consecrated in 1845 (25).
41. First Baptist Meeting House	At the Strand Street end of James Street (OS:SJ341-902-).	Dr Daniel Fabius' house might have continued as a meeting place for Protestant dissenters until his death in 1718.
77. St George's Church	On Castle site in Derby Square (OS:SJ34269028).	The authorities had considered the site as suitable for a church before Liverpool was made a parish in 1699, but the site became available only after 1718 (26). The plans for St George's were passed in 1726 and the Church itself completed in 1734. It was designed by Thomas Steers, the engineer of the first Dock (27). It was closed in 1897 and demolished in 1899 (28).
78. Benn's Garden Presbyterian Chapel	Between Red Cross Street and Canning Place (OS:SJ34269010).	This was the new site for the Castle Hey congregation's chapel from 1727. In 1811 the congregation moved to a new chapel in Renshaw Street. The Benn's Garden building was used by Welsh Wesleyan Methodists until 1866, when it was sold and used for commercial purposes (29).
79. Second Baptist Meeting House	Junction of Byrom Street and Dale Street (OS:SJ3475 9080).	This new building was opened in 1722 by the Baptists who had been meeting in Everton since 1700. The congregation moved to a large building nearby in 1789 and the old chapel was bought by the Church of England and consecrated to St Stephen. It was pulled down in the 1860s (30).
80. St Thomas' Church	Under junction of Paradise Street, Park Lane and Liver Street (OS:SJ 34518982).	The church, designed by Henry Sephton, stood on an island site between Park Lane and Cleveland Square. The foundation stone was laid in 1748 and the church was consecrated in 1750. In 1757, part of the spire was blown down and in 1783 it was hit by lightning. In 1822 the spire was taken down completely. The church was closed in 1905 and all the burials removed from the churchyard except that of Joseph Williamson, the Mole of Edge Hill (31).

George I-George III Gazetteer

Name	Location	Description
81. Octagon Chapel	North side of Victoria Street at the junction with Stanley Street (OS:SJ 34469048).	This chapel was opened in 1763 by dissenters from Key Street and Benn's Garden Chapels who wished to worship with a prayer book. It was used till 1772, after which date it was sold to the Church of England and became St Catherine's church. It was demolished in 1820 (32).
82. Third Baptist Meeting House	East side of Stanley Street, on the site of the Met. Quarter (OS:SJ34539042).	This was an off-shoot of the Baptist Chapel in Byrom Street, which was erected in 1747. The congregation moved to Comus Street in 1800 (33).
83. Synagogue	Between Victoria street (opposite the end of Cumberland Street) and Whitechapel (OS:SJ34509048).	There is some uncertainty about the date when the first synagogue was opened but it is believed to have been some time before 1775. There appears to have been a small graveyard attached to it as fragments of gravestones with Hebrew inscriptions have been found. The last interment was made before 1800 (34).
84. New Burying Ground	Underneath St John's Gardens (OS:SJ44879064).	A portion of the 'Great Heath' west of the Infirmary was enclosed and made into a burying ground with a small chapel in 1769. St John's Church was opened in 1784. The churchyard was closed in 1854 (35).
85. St Paul's Church	Under new development at north end of Bixteth Street (OS:SJ34049086).	St Paul's Square was laid out in 1760; the church was begun in 1763 and completed in 1769 to a design of Timothy Lightoler . It was demolished in 1931 and Liverpool Stadium was later built on the site (36). Recent development (2005-06) on the site has turned up some stones thought to be from one end of the church (37).
86. Pitt Street Methodist Chapel	Between Forrest Street and Surrey Street on line of Pitt Street (OS:SJ34688972).	The chapel was built in 1750, enlarged 1765, rebuilt in 1803, and altered in 1875; John Wesley preached here for a week in 1758. It appears on the 1908 OS map described as 'unused' (38).

Commerce

Name	Location	Description
8. Granary	Near the Water Street end of Rumford Street (OS:SJ341-904-).	See Medieval, Tudor, Early Stuart and Commonwealth and Later Stuart gazetteers.
9. Tithe barn	Close to the junction of Marybone and Great Crosshall Street (OS:SJ344-009-).	There are two views of a stone barn close to the given location that was not demolished until 1820, and some authorities identify it with the Tithe barn (39).
42. First Custom House	North side of Moor Street, close to the shore end (OS:SJ341902-).	See Later Stuart gazetteer

George I-George III Gazetteer

Name	Location	Description
43. Second Custom House	At the south corner of Water Street and The Strand, opposite the site of the Tower (OS:SJ34029036).	The building continued in use as a Custom House until 1722 (40), and is shown on the Bucks' view of 1728. It was demolished in 1785 when the Goree Warehouses were built on the site (41).
169. Third Custom House	East side of Canning Place (OS:SJ34478999).	This building is often referred to as the Fourth Custom House. The numbering in this gazetteer is different as the very first Custom House was located within a building with another purpose. The Town Book entry of 10 February 1717 ordered an enquiry into the possibility of building a Custom House at the dock. The brick and stone structure was built during 1721-22 and was designed by Thomas Ripley (42). It is shown on the Bucks' view of 1728. It was demolished when the old dock was filled in and the later Custom House built on the site in 1828 (43).

Docks

Name	Location	Description
44. Dock: Wet	Canning Place (OS:SJ34388996).	Nicholas Blundell, in his Diaries, recorded on the 31 August 1715 that he had seen the first three ships in the dock (44). In 1716 a second Act of Parliament was obtained to extend the time for completion of the dock and to raise the necessary funds (45). The Old Dock was finally closed in 1826 (46) and filled in to enable the construction of the new Custom House on the site in 1828.
45. Dry Dock (Small Graving Dock)	Canning Dock (OS:SJ23238996).	This graving dock appears to have been absorbed during the construction of the Dry Dock (Canning Dock) circa 1740 (47).
87. Dock: Dry	Site of Canning Dock: (OS:SJ34178997).	An entrance basin of some sort was probably built in conjunction with the original wet dock. As early as 1718, there were plans to enlarge this outer basin and provide an additional wet dock (48). It was not until 1737 that an Act of Parliament was obtained to enable the Dry Dock to be constructed (49). Construction does not appear to have started much before 1740 and was completed by 1746. The Act of 1811 allowed the Dry Dock to be converted to a wet dock but work was delayed until 1826 and was completed by 1829. The dock was renamed Canning Dock in 1832 (50).
88. Slipway	Canning Dock (OS:SJ34089017).	This is shown on Perry's plan in the north east corner of the Dry Dock at the bottom of Redcross Street.

George I-George III Gazetteer

Name	Location	Description
89. Dock: South	Site of Salthouse Dock (OS:SJ34288927).	The 1737 Dock Act provided for the construction of a wet dock to the south of the Dry Dock. Additional finance, obtained in April 1745, enabled construction on the south side of the entrance to the Old Dock to commence but it was 1749 before shipbuilders, who occupied much of the site, were given notice to quit. The South Dock was not finished until 1754, when the Corporation advanced a further £1000 to the Trustees to enable them to complete it (51). The Dock was renamed Salthouse Dock in about 1784 and reconstructed in 1845 (52).
90. Dock: Dry (Graving Dock)	East side of Canning Half-Tide Dock (OS:SJ34068987).	In 1756, a third graving dock was built to the westwards of the new entrance to the South Dock (Salthouse Dock) (53).
91. Dock: Dry (Graving Dock)	Canning Graving Docks (OS:SJ34022897).	Two further graving docks were constructed on the west side of the Dry Dock (Canning) between 1765 and 1769. Although subsequently modified, these two graving docks are still in existence (54).
92. Dock: Dry (Graving Dock)	Mann Island (OS:SJ34069010).	This is the dock shown on Perry's plan as north of Nova Scotia. A new graving dock was constructed at the north end of the new Dry Dock (Canning) in 1746. This site was later reconstructed as George's Dock Passage (55).
93. Dock: New (George's Dock)	Mann Island to St Nicholas Place (OS:SJ33949092).	The Dock Act of 1761 permitted the construction of a new wet dock to the north of the Dry Dock (Canning Dock). A start was made in 1762 but the works were destroyed in a storm and it was not until 1767 that a new foundation stone was laid. The dock, later to be named George's Dock, was completed in 1771. George's Dock underwent various alterations in the 19th century and was finally closed in 1900 (56).
94. Dock: New Dry (George's Dock Basin)	St Nicholas Place (OS:SJ33869041).	It is presumed that the tidal basin at the north end of the new dock (George's), sanctioned by the Act of 1761, was constructed and completed at the same time as the new dock in 1771. The entrance basin was closed in 1871 (57).

Industry
Mills

10. Eastham Dale Water Mill	Close to site of John Moores University, Byrom Street campus (OS:SJ348-911--).	See Medieval gazetteer.
11. Eastham Wind Mill	On high ground north west of junction of Gerard Street and Christian Street (OS: SJ349- 910-).	See Medieval and Tudor, Early Stuart and Commonwealth gazetteers.

George I-George III Gazetteer

Name	Location	Description
12. Horse Mill (1)	North west of Old Moore Hall in an area west of Old Hall Street and north of Union Street (OS:SJ338-907-).	See Medieval and Tudor, Early Stuart and Commonwealth gazetteers.
13. Townsend Mill	On the site of the Steble fountain in front of the Walker Art Gallery (OS:SJ35009074).	The mill was included in the Moore estate purchased by Lord Derby in 1724. The Corporation obtained it in 1780 and shortly afterwards it was demolished (58). It is not shown on Charles Eyes' plan of 1785.
14. Horse Mill (2)	Near south corner of junction of Brunswick Street and Castle Street (OS:SJ34229036).	See Later Stuart gazetteer.
21. Water Mill	In the area between Stafford Street and Audley Street, close to London Road (OS:SJ357-907-).	The mill was being worked in 1716. Subsequently it was used as a seed mill until 1750. The mill pool itself is shown on Charles Eyes' plan of 1785 (59).
22. Middle Mill (1)	On high ground north of Dale Street between Johnson Street and North Street (OS:SJ34569086).	The mill is marked clearly on Yates' and Perry's plan of 1768 (60) and on Perry's plan of 1769. It is not shown on Charles Eyes' plan of 1785.
46. Horse Mill (3)	Derby Square (OS:SJ3426 9027).	See Later Stuart gazetteer.
47. Horse Mill (4)	Castle Street.	See Later Stuart gazetteer.
48. Horse Mill (5)	High Street.	See Later Stuart gazetteer.
49. Middle Mill (2)	North of Dale Street, on the west side of Trueman Street (OS:SJ34619084).	This mill is shown clearly on Yates' and Perry's plan of 1768 (61) and on Perry's plan of 1769, but it is not shown on Charles Eyes' plan of 1785.
50. Oil Mill	On the site of St George's Hall (OS:SJ349-906-).	The Infirmary was constructed on Oyl Mill field and some waste land adjoining it at the top of Shaw's Brow in 1744-45.
51. Paul's Mill	Corner of Smithfield Street and Cockspur Street (OS:SJ34289094).	The mill is indicated on Yates' and Perry's plan of 1768 (62) and Perry's plan of 1769, but not on Charles Eyes' plan of 1785.
52. Park Mill	To the west of the junction between Park Lane and Jamaica Street (OS:SJ34758942).	The mill appears on Yates' and Perry's plan of 1768 (63) and on Perry's plan of 1769, but not on Charles Eyes' plan of 1785.

George I-George III Gazetteer

Name	Location	Description
95. Gallows Mill (1)	Junction of Stafford Street and London Road (OS:SJ35449074).	This was built in 1715 on a lane leading towards Mr Norris' mill and a few months later in 1716 four Jacobite rebels were hanged, drawn and quartered near it. It was bought by the Corporation in 1788 in order to be demolished (64). It is shown on Gore's plan of 1796 but not on Horwood's plan of 1803.
96. Mill	36 to 58 Brownlow Hill (OS:SJ35359025).	A mill associated with Liverpool China Factory (65) (see site 119)
97. Gallows Mill (2)	Near junction of Gildart Street and Constance Street (OS:SJ355-908-).	The mill was built in 1719 by Alderman Tyrer who had a lease for 3 lives and a 21 year lease. By 1757 it had passed to Samuel Jones and by 1774 to William Farrington (66). It is marked on Gore's plan of 1796, but not on Horwood's of 1803.
98. Appleton's Mill	South side of Upper Duke Street, opposite the end of Pilgrim Street (OS:SJ35398958).	This mill had been built on Cathedral Mount (Quarry Hill) by 1723 when Edward Appleton proposed to buy the Mill that he had been leasing. By 1766 it was known as Thomas Appleton's Mill and it was mentioned in 1782. In 1805 the death of the miller Edward Haighton was reported (67). It is shown on Sherwood's plan of 1821, but not on Gage's plan of 1835.
99. Windmill	South east corner of present Salthouse Dock/Gower Street (OS:SJ34428968).	There was a windmill in the yard of Mr Backham's salt works on the seaward side (68).
100. Windmill	Lime Street Station next to Skelhorne Street (OS:SJ35069048).	Shown on Perry's plan of 1769 next to the rope works. Shown on Eyes' map of 1785 but not on Horwood's map dated 1803.
101. Mill	North of William Brown Street (OS:SJ35019075).	Shown on Perry's plan of 1769 off Shaw's Brow but not on Eyes' plan of 1785.
102. Taylor's Mill	North of William Brown Street (OS:SJ34949078).	Owned by Thomas Taylor, a corn-factor, who died in 1780 and then leased by William and Robert Taylor. Raised to a "very great height at considerable expense" in 1784. Between 1813-15 it ground flour and peas for Wellington's army. It burnt down in 1824 (65). Shown on Perry's plan of 1769 across the road from Townsend Mill off Shaw's Brow but not on Eyes' plan of 1785.

Salt

23. Salt House	North side of Chapel Street, at the junction with New Quay (OS:SJ33929053).	See Later Stuart gazetteer.
53. Saltworks	East quay of present Salthouse Dock (OS:SJ34428973).	The saltworks are shown on Perry's plan of 1769. By the late eighteenth century complaints about the smoke and steam emitted led to its closure in 1793. The Blackburns relocated the Works to Garston Creek (69).

George I-George III Gazetteer

Name	Location	Description
Sugar		
54. Sugar House	Close to north west corner of junction of Redcross Street and Derby Square (OS:SJ34259022).	The building is clearly marked on Perry's plan of 1769, but not on subsequent plans. Gore lists two sugar bakers in Redcross Street in 1766. Mawer gives 3 sugar houses in Redcross Street as follows: 1673 Smith, Cleveland, and Danvers; 1766 Oldham, Caldwell & Co, and Wakefield, Thomas & Co, both sugar bakers. It is not clear which ones were at this site, or whether they all were. The *Weekly Courant* newspaper states that a fire, assumed to be at this site, consumed the building in August 1750, and says that a similar destruction by fire happened about 25 years earlier, in about 1725 (70).
55. Sugar House	North side of Union Court and west of North John Street (OS: SJ3430 9044).	It is shown on Perry's plan of 1769. Gore's Directory gives a sugar house in between John Street and Castle Street occupied by John Tarleton & Co in 1766. It seems to be on Horwood's map of 1803, though not named on it.
56. Sugar Refinery	North west corner of Harrington Street and North John Street (OS:SJ34409035).	The site is found on Perry's plan of 1769. Gore's Directory names John Knight & Co as occupying the site as sugar bakers in 1766. It seems to be on Horwood's map of 1803, but it is not named on it.
103. Cleveland Square Sugar House	Corner of Henry Street, Argyll Street, and Campbell Street (OS:SJ34648989).	Found on Perry's plan of 1769. It was occupied by Joseph Harvey, sugar baker, in 1766 according to Gore's Directory. Not on Horwood's plan of 1803
104. Sugarhouse Yard	East Side of Strand Street (OS:SJ34229008).	Shown on Perry's plan of 1769 and Eyes map of 1765. Shown as Mr. Bold's Sugar House on Horwood's plan of 1803.
105. Hughes Sugar House	Between Victoria Street and Matthew Street (OS:SJ34439043).	Found on Perry's plan of 1769, and named as Hughes Sugar House. Gore's Directory names Richard Hughes & Co as occupying the site in 1766. Not on Horwood's plan of 1803.
106. Sugar House	Old Haymarket (OS:SJ34749072).	Found on Perry's plan of 1769. Gore's Directory says a sugar house in Dale Street is occupied by Blundell, Jonathan & Co, Haymarket in 1766. Shown as the Old Sugar House on Horwood's plan dated 1803.
107. Sugar House	Duke St, just north east of Argyll Street (OS:SJ34638989).	Gore's Directory lists a sugar house in Duke Street occupied by George Campbell, Sen. & Co in 1766.

George I-George III Gazetteer

Name	Location	Description
Dying & tanning		
57. Dye Works	South west of Gilbert Street on line of Greetham Street (OS:SJ34778975).	The building is shown on Perry's plan of 1769 as "out in Mr Seel's fields". It is marked but not named on Gore's 1796 plan. It is not shown on Horwood's plan of 1803.
58. Tannery	West side of Hatton Garden behind the Magistrates Court in Dale Street (OS:SJ34469080).	The site continued to be used. It is marked on Perry's plan of 1769 and on Horwood's plan of 1803, but not on Sherwood's plan of 1821.
59. Tannery	Lord Street (OS:SJ 34489078).	See Later Stuart gazetteer.
108. Mr Mort's Tanyard	Between Haymarket and Spitalfields (OS:SJ34699068).	Shown on Perry's plan of 1769. Gore's Directory shows George Mort as a tanner and skinner, located in the Haymarket in 1766.
109. Skinner's Yard	Cheapside, off Dale Street (OS:SJ34489078).	Shown on Perry's plan of 1769 next to a tan yard. Gore's Directory shows John Chorley and James Woods as Tanners in Cheapside (Dale Street) in 1766.
110. Tanyard	Under Byrom Street some 320m to the north of Queensway Tunnel entrance (OS:SJ34929107).	Shown on Perry's plan of 1769.
Pot Works		
60. Pot Works	North west corner of Lord Street and Whitechapel (OS:SJ34549031).	Josiah Poole's pottery continued in use throughout the period (71). It is not, however, shown on Perry's plan of 1769.
111. Pot Works	East side of southern end of Trueman Street (OS:SJ34659083).	George Walker and Jos. Mercer leased the site for a house and pot house in 1718. It was sold in 1724 by Mr John Douse to James Shaw. It is shown on Perry's plan of 1769 as 'Mr. Shaw's Pot House'. The site was occupied by a dwelling house in 1785 (72).
112. Pot Works	Site of Liverpool Central Libraries, William Brown Street (OS :SJ34899079).	Shown on Perry's plan of 1769. According to Walker Art Gallery Decorative Arts department, this is the upper Shaw's Brow Pottery, belonging to Samuel Gilbody and Thomas Morris from 1714-1756 and to Samuel Gilbody (the son) from 1756-1761. Gore's Directory lists Charles Woods & Co, Mug makers in Shaw's Brow in 1766, with four other potters and a china manufacturer. By 1802 the premises were used for a soap and candle factory (73). This site is shown but not named on Horwood's map of 1803. It may have grown to include the pot works just downhill.

George I-George III Gazetteer

Name	Location	Description
113. Pot Works	Site now occupied by west end of World Museum Liverpool (OS:SJ 34859080).	North of Shaw's Brow. Shown on Perry's plan of 1769. Known as Richard Chaffer's Pot House from about 1752 . Walker Art Gallery Decorative Arts Department says that R. Chaffers & Co produced porcelain from 1755-1765, with other potters at this site until after 1799, including Seth Pennington and John Part (1776-1799), followed by Pennington and Edwards (74). Several other potters are known to have operated in Shaw's Brow as listed in Gore's Directory for 1766. Although this site is not shown separately on Horwood's map of 1803, the drawing is consistent with its incorporation in the pot-house just uphill.
114. Pot Works	Corner of St James Street and Blundell Street. (OS:SJ34828947).	Shown on Perry's plan of 1769 at the south-east end of Park Lane. Richard Thwaites, potter, is listed in Gore's Directory for 1766 in Park Lane.
115. Pot Works	Gradwell Street (OS:SJ 34728998).	Pothouse lane connected Duke Street and Wolstenholme Street (later Gradwell Street) on Perry's plan of 1769. A tin-glazed earthenware pottery house is noted in Pothouse Lane in the early eighteenth century. Gore's Directory lists George Drinkwater & Co, Potters, in Duke Street in 1766, while James Drinkwater is also said to have manufactured coarseware, smeared with thick tin glaze and ornamented with blue painted Chinese-type figures, at this site (75). A brewery is shown on this site on Horwood's map of 1803.
116. Pot Works	Under Queensway Tunnel entrance (OS:SJ34749074).	Shown on Perry's plan of 1769. Gore's Directory lists James Cotter and Son as potters in Haymarket in 1766. This may be the pottery on the south side of Dale Street (76). Horwood's map of 1803 shows a merchant's house located at this site.
117. Pot Works	Corner of North Street and Dale Street (OS:SJ34649077).	Shown on Perry's plan of 1769. An old plan of Liverpool, dated 1760, shows a pottery on this site and mentions two other potteries in Dale Street (77). Horwood's map of 1803 shows a brewery and houses on this site.
118. Mr Livesley's Mughouse	Under Byrom Street some 360 metres north of Queensway Tunnel entrance (OS:SJ34829111).	Shown on Perry's plan of 1769. Not shown on Horwood's map of 1803.

George I-George III Gazetteer

Name	Location	Description
119. Liverpool China Manufactory	36 to 58 Brownlow Hill (OS:SJ35359025).	It is shown on Charles Eyes' map of 1765 but is beyond the scope of Perry's plan. William Reid's china factory produced blue and white porcelain from late 1756 until 1761 (78). James Pennington and others produced pottery on this site until 1768. Archaeological excavation in 1997-98 showed the base of the factory and of a mill for grinding colours, as well as structures which may be associated with kiln flues. The excavations recovered large quantities of kiln brick, saggar and other kiln furniture and many tiny fragments of biscuit ware and porcelain. By 1803 the plot was vacant.
Glass works		
120. Glass Works	Corner of Argyle Street and Paradise Street (OS:SJ3456 8993).	Mr Josiah Poole opened a glasshouse in 1715. Messers Crosbie, Bostock, & Co. are listed in Gore's Directory in 1766 under Hanover Street. It is shown on the Bucks' view of 1728. Nicholas Blundell took his daughters to see it in 1723 (79). Shown on Perry's plan of 1769 with a chimney indicated. It was occupied by Crown Glass (T. Holt) in 1781. Charles Eyes' Map of 1785 shows small terraced houses on this site (80).
121. Glass Works	Wapping Basin quayside (OS:SJ34428961).	It was built in 1759 by John Knight & Co. It is shown on Perry's plan of 1769 with a chimney indicated, as the New Glasshouse in South Dock. It had been recently completed in 1769. Gore's Directory lists John Knight & Co, Glassmakers, on the north-east side of South Dock in 1766. The ownership changed in 1769 and after 1779 there was a bottle house here, owned by Leigh & Co. It is not shown on Horwood's map of 1803 (81).
122. Glass Works	To the west of Vernon Street (OS:SJ34359071).	A short-lived glass factory consisting of two glasshouses making fine flint glass was started before 1758 in Dale Street. This site, Glasshouse Wient, is off Dale Street, and may well be the site referred to. John and William Penkett occupied the site from 1756 to 1759 and the site was unlet in 1761. No glass manufacturers are listed in Gore's Directory in Glasshouse Wient in 1766. Shown on Perry's plan of 1769 with a chimney indicated (82).
Silk		
123. Silkhouse	North side of Victoria Street under Carlisle Buildings (OS:SJ34689061).	Shown on Perry's plan of 1769. Gore's Directory notes Fairfax, Scarratt, & Co, Silk Weavers, in Spitalfields under 'Whitechapel' in 1766.
124. Silkhouse	Site of Silkhouse Court in Tithebarn Street.	Shown on Perry's plan of 1769. Thomas Hopkins of London established the first Liverpool silkhouse in Silkhouse Lane, off Tithebarn Street, in 1753. Thomas Hopkins & Co., Silk throwsters, are listed in Tithebarn Street in Gore's Directory in 1766. Horwood's map of 1803 shows cottages at this site (83).

George I-George III Gazetteer

Name	Location	Description
Brewing & Distilling		
125. Brewery	South side of Duke Street close to the junction with Suffolk Street (OS:SJ34869083).	Shown on Perry's plan of 1769. Leigh, Ross & Co, brewers, are listed in Duke Street in Gore's Directory for 1766.
126. Brewery	South side of Fleet Street (OS:SJ34849008).	Shown on Perry's plan of 1769. Two brewers are listed in Fleet Street in Gore's Directory for 1766, James Eyes, and Pearson, Allan & Co. Shown as Mr. Unsworth's brewery on Horwood's plan of 1803.
127. Mr Crosbie's Brewery	Corner of Seel Street and Concert Street (OS:SJ34948996).	Shown on Perry's plan of 1769 on the west side of Fleet Street as Mr Crosbie's Brewery. Shown as Mr. Taylor's brewery on Horwood's plan of 1803.
128. Brewery	South of Renshaw Street on the corner of Ranelagh Street (OS:SJ35049024).	Shown on Perry's plan of 1769. Thomas Jennion, brewer, is listed in Gore's Directory for 1766 in Ranelagh Street.
129. Brewery	Between north end of Tithebarn Street and Cockspur Street (OS:SJ34369092).	Shown on Perry's plan of 1769. Thomas Payne, brewer, is listed in Gore's Directory for Milk Street in 1766. A brewery still existed on the site in 1850.
130. Distillery	South of Sir Thomas Street at junction with Victoria Street (OS:SJ34559049).	Shown on Perry's plan of 1769. Green & Longden, distillers, are listed in Gore's Directory for 1766 in St Thomas's Buildings.
Ropewalks		
61. Old Ropery Rope Works	Old Ropery Street (OS:SJ34149028).	Not shown on Chadwick's plan of 1725 but its location and alignment is indicated on John Eyes' 1765 plan by Old Ropery Street running west from Fenwick Street. See also the Dry Bridge, site 72.
62. Rope Works: Ladies Walk North	Between Old Hall Street and Bath Street, north of Brook Street (OS:SJ33869084).	Shown on John Eyes' 1765 plan and named Ladies Walk on Perry's 1769 plan and on Charles Eyes' 1785 plan.
63. Rope Works	Cable Street under the Grosvenor Development (2007) (OS:SJ34369022).	Shown as Cable Street on the Chadwick plan of 1725.
131. Rope Works	Between Sir Thomas Street and Cumberland Street from Whitechapel to Dale Street (OS:SJ34509058).	Shown as Rope Yard running between Dale Street and an unnamed road on the Chadwick plan of 1725. Built over by the time of John Eyes' 1765 plan.

Name	Location	Description
132. Rope Works: Ladies Walk South	Duke Street (north side) from opposite east end of Wolstenholme Square to Colquitt Street (OS:SJ34918989).	The site appears unnamed on the Chadwick plan of 1725. In 1763 the Corporation purchased the site from Alderman Gildart to make it into a public walk known later as the (South) Ladies Walk (84). On John Eyes' plan of 1765 the site is occupied by a Ladies Walk, adjacent to Duke Street and an Old Ropery. Built over by the time of Kaye's 1816 plan.
133. Rope Walk	North side of Renshaw Street (OS:SJ35129014).	It is shown as a ropery on John Eyes' 1765 plan and Perry's 1769 plan. It was built over by the time of Charles Eyes' 1785 plan. John and Edward Renshaw owned a ropery on the site in the eighteenth century (85).
134. Rope Works: White Ropery	Hawke Street between Brownlow Hill and Copperas Street (OS:SJ35199033).	Marked as White Ropery on John Eyes' 1765 plan and the Perry plan of 1769. On Charles Eyes' 1785 plan the site is named for a Mr Brown but not identified as a Rope Works. By the time of Kaye's plan dated 1816 Hawke Street had replaced the rope works .
135. Rope Works	Junction of Lime Street and Skelhorne Street running east under Lime Street Station (OS:SJ35069046).	It is shown as a Ropery on John Eyes' 1765 plan and a Rope Walk on the Perry plan of 1769. Shown as built over on Kaye's plan of 1816.
136. Rope Works	Between William Brown Street and St John's Lane alongside St George's Hall (OS:SJ34909058).	John Eyes' 1765 plan shows two unidentified parallel walks beside the Infirmary and its garden. Perry's plan names the western walk as a White Ropery. On Horwood's 1803 plan the western walk is now Mr Coventry (sic) Ropery while the Lunatic Asylum occupies the eastern site (86). On Kaye's plan of 1810 the western walk's site is still shown but not identified.
137. Rope Works	Queens Square to Ranelagh Street under St John's Centre and Clayton Square (OS:SJ34879049).	The site is shown on Chadwick's plan of 1725. Horwood's map of 1803 names Mr Dean's and Mr Platt's Roperies. They are still identified as roperies on Kaye's plan of 1816.
138. Rope Works	Great Charlotte Street (OS:SJ34969026).	Identified as a White Ropery on John Eyes' 1765 plan and on Perry's plan of 1769. It is not shown on Charles Eyes' 1785 plan.

George I-George III Gazetteer

Name	Location	Description
139. Rope Walk	Bold Street (OS:SJ34978999).	John Eyes' plan of 1765 shows three parallel walks each identified as Ropery. Perry's plan of 1769 names them from east to west as Mr Brown's, Chas Goore Esq's and Mr Brooke's Rope Walks. By Charles Eyes' 1785 plan these walks have been replaced by Bold Street and two further walks have appeared parallel to Bold Street approximately along the line of the railway into Central Station. On Horwood's 1803 plan these are named Mr Stamforth's and Messrs Johnson and Machell's Roperies and are bridged over by Newington. They survive onto the Kaye plan of 1816. Jonas Bold, who had the lease of the land in the 18th century, gave his name to Bold Street (87).
140. Rope Works	Berry Street from Bold Street to Duke Street (OS:SJ35208979).	Shown as Rope Walk on the Perry plan of 1769. On Charles Eyes' 1785 plan it has been replaced by a street named as Colquitt Street. By the Kaye 1816 plan this street is renamed Berry Street and the name 'Colquitt' has been transferred to its present location.
141. Rope Works	Blundell Street (OS:SJ34788942).	Shown as a White Ropery on John Eyes' 1765 plan and on Perry's plan of 1769. By Charles Eyes' 1785 plan it had been overlaid by Blundell Street.
142. Rope Works	Parallel to and between Sparling Street and Kings Dock Street (OS:SJ34698947).	On John Eyes' plan of 1765 it is shown as 'Ropery' running from Upper Park Lane down to the South Shore alongside a large garden. On Perry's plan of 1769 the walk is named Messrs Crosbies and Sidall's Ropery and the garden is named as Mr Critchley's Garden. On Charles Eyes' 1765 plan there are three parallel walks and the South Shore is now Wapping, while on Horwood's 1803 plan these are named, from north to south, as Messrs B and T Greetham's, Mr Priestman's, and Mr Molyneux's Roperies. A single walk remains on Kaye's plan of 1816.
143. Rope Works	On line of Queens Dock Street between Park Lane and Wapping.	Shown as Ropery on John Eyes' 1765 plan. On Perry's plan of 1769 it appears to have been overlaid by Mason Street.

Other Sites

Name	Location	Description
144. Battery and Magazine	George's Dock gates (OS:SJ33939045).	The battery is shown on Perry's plan of 1769. The Vestry Books show in 1759 that a fortification was ordered in the new part of St Nicholas church and in 1760 the churchyard was surveyed. There was an order in 1772 to level the battery and to add the land to the churchyard. For some time the powder magazine for the battery was used as a lock-up or bridewell. A building that could be the magazine appears on Charles Eyes' plan of 1785. In 1804 the building was demolished when the bridewell was transferred to the South Chapel (88).

George I-George III Gazetteer

Name	Location	Description
145. Powder Magazine	Brownlow Hill, opposite north end of Clarence Street (OS:SJ35419032).	In 1737 a magazine for storing gunpowder on the north side of Brownlow Hill Lane was leased to Thomas Pearse, Samuel Underhill and Robert Norman. In 1751 it moved to Liscard across the Mersey. The site is off Perry's plan of 1769 but appears on Charles Eyes' map of 1785. It has been replaced by Russell Street on Kaye's 1810 plan. The building was used to hold prisoners of the French and American revolutionary wars (89).
146. Watch House and Powder Magazine	Corner of Rodney Street and Upper Duke Street (OS:SJ35368960).	These sites must have been in existence before 1768 because in that year the Town Book ordered the Powder Magazine and Watch House to be pulled down and rebuilt in another place and the site to be converted into a Bowling Green (90).
147. Turpentine Works	Brownlow Hill (OS:SJ35509032).	Shown on John Eyes' Plan of 1765. It covered three old Powder Magazines, two lamp black houses and a resin house. At an unknown date it was converted into Joseph Brook's Pot Works (91).
148. Copper Works	South east corner of Wapping Docks (OS:SJ34388971).	Shown on Perry's plan of 1769. It opened in 1768 and moved in 1791 after a legal case about damage to the surrounding gardens. In the 1790s it closed when the rising cost of coal made it more economic for the works to be located nearer the coal fields (92).
149. Iron Foundry	South of Sir Thomas Street near junction with Victoria Street (OS:SJ35439074).	Shown on Perry's plan of 1769. There was a coal-yard in Sir Thomas Street next to the foundry.
150. Iron Foundry	In Lydia Anne Street (OS:SJ34758979).	Shown on Perry's plan of 1769. The foundry was opened shortly after 1758. The foundry later became the Phoenix Foundry (93).
151. Iron Foundry	South west corner of Albert Dock (OS:SJ34218971).	Shown on Perry's plan of 1769.
152. Limekilns	South side of Bold Street under Central Station shopping area (OS:SJ34929017).	Shown on Perry's plan of 1769 next to the three Bold Street ropeworks.
153. Limekilns	Between Byrom Street and the south end of Fontenoy Street (OS:SJ34749083).	Shown on Perry's plan of 1769.
154. Limekilns	At the junction of Brook Street and New Quay (OS:SJ33849073).	Shown on Perry's plan of 1769 on the west side of Mr Brook's brickyard.

George I-George III Gazetteer

Name	Location	Description
155. Brickyard	Either side of Brook Street between Old Hall Street and New Quay (OS:SJ33859076).	Shown on Perry's plan of 1769. Mr Brook's brickyard disappeared when the Leeds and Liverpool canal basin opened in the Old Hall Street area in 1774. It gave its name to Brook Street (94).
156. The Baths	West side of Bath Street/ Princes Dock development (OS:SJ33659093).	Erected on the North Key about 1765 by ship-builder John Naylor Wright or his father. In 1794 the Corporation bought the baths and improved them at a cost of £1000. About 1817 they were moved to accomodate Princes Dock. Public baths are shown on Eyes' plan of 1765 and on Perry's plan of 1769 (95).
157. Machine	North side of junction at Brook Street and New Quay (OS:SJ33819076).	Shown on Perry's plan of 1769. This may be a water pump associated with the Baths.
158. Boatyard	North of Bath Street near the south end of Gibralter Row (OS:SJ33729086).	Shown on Perry's plan of 1769. William Dutton opened his boatyard about 1760. It disappeared when the Leeds and Liverpool canal basin opened in Old Hall Street in 1774. It gave its name to Dutton Street which was cut through from Mill Lane (Great Howard Street) in about 1780 (96).
159. Brickyard	To west of Dale Street between Byrom Street and Hatton Garden (OS:SJ34619089).	Shown on Perry's plan of 1769 in fields west of Dale Street as a brick and tile-making site known as Thomas Grasse's brickyard (97).
160. Marble yard	Queens Square (OS:SJ34739050).	Shown on Perry's plan of 1769.
161. Machine	Under entrance to Queensway Tunnel (OS:SJ34749066).	Shown on Perry's plan of 1769.
162. Ranelagh Pleasure Gardens	Under present Adelphi Hotel (OS:SJ35159031).	A house of entertainment was established at the White House in about 1722. There is some uncertainty as to whether the gardens opened at the same time or not until 1759. The name of the gardens was copied from a London establishment. They contained a fish-pond and a pavilion that acted as a bandstand (98).
163. Library	Various locations.	In 1758 the members of the Conversation Club decided to establish a general circulating library in Princes Street It moved to North John Street in 1759, to Lord Street in 1787, and to the present Lyceum Building in Bold Street in 1803. A short-lived attempt was made in 1769 to set up an Academy of Painting in connection with the Library but the scheme was abandoned after a few months, revived in 1773, and suspended during the Napoleonic Wars (99).

Name	Location	Description
Charitable Institutions		
24. Pool House	Under the Queen Elizabeth II Law Courts (OS:SJ343-900-).	It was pulled down in 1804 (100).
164. Workhouse or Poor House	On the corner of College Lane and Hanover Street (OS:SJ34729011).	The first appearance of a poor house seems to have been in 1723, when the overseers of the poor agreed to take 36 new houses erected by Bryan Blundell on the south side of the Charity School. The Workhouse was built in 1732 on the same site to replace the old Poor House which had become inadequate. It was replaced by a new workhouse on Brownlow Hill in 1770 (101).
Almshouses		
64. Poole's Almshouses	South side of William Brown Street near the foot of St John's Gardens (OS:SJ34829073).	They form part of the building numbered 59 on Chadwick's 1725 map. By 1748 they had become dilapidated and were demolished and replaced by a set built near the Fall Well (102). In 1787 the various different almshouses in the town were demolished and new ones were built in Cambridge Street near the top of Mount Pleasant in 1788 (103).
65. Richmond's Almshouses	South side of William Brown Street, near the foot of St John's Gardens (OS:SJ34829073).	In 1723, John Scarsbrick, Mayor, gave £70 towards completing Richmond's Almshouses (104). They form part of the building numbered 59 on Chadwick's 1725 map. In 1749 three sets of almshouses were demolished and replaced by the set built near the Fall Well (102). In 1787 the various different almshouses in the town were demolished and new ones were built in Cambridge Street near the top of Mount Pleasant in 1788 (103).
66. Warbrick's Almshouses	At the junction of Bold Street and Hanover Street (OS:SJ34849018).	These almshouses continued in use until their demolition in 1787. They were replaced by the new set in Cambridge Street near the top of Mount Pleasant in 1788 (103).
165. Scarsbrick's Almshouses	South side of William Brown Street, near the foot of St John's Gardens (OS:SJ34829073).	James Scarsbrick, brother of John, died in 1724 and left money to build almshouses for sailors' widows. Another block was erected east of the almshouses at the Dale Street end. In 1733 the demolition of one of the almshouses next to Richmond's was ordered to allow a passage to the Ormskirk Road, and the materials were to be set up at the other end so that the accommodation would not be lost (105). In 1749 three sets of almshouses were demolished and replaced by the set built near the Fall Well (102). These are shown on Perry's 1769 plan, but the same plan also clearly marks structures on the original site and names two of them as almshouses. They are not named as such on later plans and some, if not all of the buildings on the site had been demolished by the time of Horwood's plan of 1803.

George I-George III Gazetteer

Name	Location	Description
Schools		
67. Charity School	South side of School Lane, east of Bluecoat Chambers (OS:SJ34739016).	The old Grammar School was replaced in 1718 by a new, purpose-built school on land which had been allocated by the Corporation close to the original site. In 1721 the Mayor visited the Free School (old Grammar School) that had been moved to School Lane from St Mary del Kaye churchyard. Perry's plan of 1769 shows a Manufactory for Stockings above the Free School, but it is not known if it was directly associated with the school. It remained a Free Charity School until 1803 (106).
68. The Bluecoat School	School Lane (OS:SJ34689015).	In 1722 a further piece of land was added and more buildings were erected (107). The Bluecoat School moved to Wavertree in 1906. Bluecoat Chambers became an Art School, then an arts centre and studios. In 2007 the buildings are currently undergoing renovation.
166. Mr Chalmers School	North of Union Street (OS:SJ33949068).	This is shown on Perry's plan of 1769. Gore's Directory for 1766 lists Sarah Chalmers, Boarding School, Union Street.
167. Independent School	Redcross Street and Cable Street (OS:SJ342962).	This school was run by William Smith and later by his son, Egerton Smith, who founded and edited the *Liverpool Mercury* (108).
168. Boarding School	Chapel Street (OS:SJ340905) approximately.	Gore's Directory for 1766 lists Alice Shaw, Boarding School.
Law & Order		
25. First Stocks	In front of the present Town Hall (OS:SJ34219047).	See Later Stuart gazetteer.
26. Pinfold	Close to junction of Cockspur Street and Vauxhall Road (OS:SJ34389097).	The pinfold is clearly marked on Perry's plan of 1769, and appears on Charles Eyes' 1785 plan but is not shown on Kaye's 1816 plan. Its use in 1784 is recorded (109).
27. First Pillory	In front of the present Town Hall (OS:SJ34219047).	See Later Stuart gazetteer.
28. Ducking Stool	South east of the junction of Great Crosshall Street and Hatton Garden (OS:SJ344-908-).	The last reference to this ducking stool was made in October 1714. However, as late as 1802 the House of Correction attracted public opprobrium for the continuing use of a ducking stool and whipping post to chastise female prisoners (110).

George I-George III Gazetteer

Name	Location	Description
69. Second Stocks	Derby Square (OS:SJ34279024).	In 1721, during his year as mayor, Bryan Blundell presented new stocks. Excavations in 1976 uncovered the remains of two slots that might have held the stocks. In 1763, Mr John Tarleton, Mayor, had the stocks removed and an obelisk erected on the site (111).
70. Second Pillory	Derby Square (OS:SJ34279024).	In 1749 the pillory was to be repaired, but in 1763 Mr John Tarleton, the Mayor, had it removed, with the stocks, and an obelisk erected on the site. It was replaced by a moveable pillory which was used until at least the end of the century (112). Excavations in 1976 found a pit which could have been used to hold the base of a whipping post (113).
71. Cage	Derby Square, close to the top of Red Cross Street (OS:SJ34279021).	Chadwick's 1725 map shows a circular structure which would seem to be the cage/lock-up provided by Bryan Blundell in 1721. It is not shown on later plans except on the Eyes' inset at the top of Horwood's plan of 1803, which purports to show Liverpool in 1725 though it was not drawn at that time. Excavations in 1976 uncovered a large circular pit that could have been the base of the cage (114).

Crosses and Sanctuary Stones
Wayside Crosses

Name	Location	Description
15. Everston Cross	West side of Bevington Hill above north slip road from Kingsway Tunnel to Scotland Road (OS:SJ347-917-).	See Medieval gazetteer.
16. White Cross	West side of Scotland Road, nearly opposite junction with Bostock Street (OS :SJ34819227).	It is shown as 'Remains of an Ancient Cross' on Sherwood's plan of 1821.
17. High Cross	Junction of Castle Street, Dale Street, High Street and Water Street (OS:SJ34219047).	See Tudor, Early Stuart and Commonwealth and Later Stuart gazetteers.
29. St Patrick's Cross	Junction of Hatton Garden, Marybone, Tithebarn Street and Vauxhall Road (OS: SJ34429092).	The cross is marked on Perry's plan of 1769, but not on later ones, although it is referred to in 1770 and 1786 (115).

Town Crosses

Name	Location	Description
18. Red Cross	Corner of Derby Square and Red Cross Street (OS:SJ34289020).	The cross is not mentioned for this period. Some authorities attribute the name 'Red Cross' to the obelisk erected by Mr John Tarleton, Mayor, in 1763 (111).
30. Townsend Cross	Close to the junction of William Brown Street and Byrom Street (OS:SJ34789078).	See Tudor, Early Stuart and Commonwealth and Later Stuart gazetteers.

George I-George III Gazetteer

Name	Location	Description
31. White Cross	Junction of Chapel Street, High Street, Old Hall Street and Tithebarn Street (OS:SJ34129059).	The cross remained intact until 1746 when it was recorded that it had been "pulled down by some evilminded persons". It was ordered to be rebuilt, but this was not done and later in the year the ruins and steps were ordered to be taken away. This had not been done by 1756 and the site clearance was again ordered. Brooke recorded in 1853 that people recently living could remember it (116). In excavations for telephone cables in 1897 three yellow stone blocks were uncovered at the site. They measured 3' x 2' x 1' and may have been the remains of the base of the cross (117).
Sanctuary Stones		
19. Castle Street	In the roadway of Castle Street near the present Town Hall, some 45 metres south of the junction with Water Street (OS:SJ34219042).	The site of the stone has never been forgotten and it can still be seen today. In 1907 it was advertised as the Liberty Stone, outside McGuffie's Dispensary & Photographic Chemists (118). In 2007 a plaque next to Furness Building Society marks the site.
20. Dale Street	In the roadway opposite the top of Stanley Street (OS: SJ34399059).	The position is clearly marked on Perry's plan of 1769, but it is not shown on later ones.
Bridges and Wells		
32. Townsend Bridge	From east end of Dale Street to west end of William Brown Street (OS:SJ34759076).	See Later Stuart gazetteer.
33. Pool Bridge	Crossing the line of Paradise Street near the junction with College Lane (OS:SJ34559011).	See Later Stuart gazetteer.
72. Dry Bridge	Across the line of Moor Street and Castle Hill between Fenwick Street and James Street (OS:SJ34199032).	In 1802 an exchange of property which involved the Corporation referred to "The Rope Walk under the Dry Bridge" (119). It is named on Perry's plan of 1769 but not on susequent ones. On Perry's plan the name covered not only the bridge itself, but also the part of Fenwick Street south of it.
73. Lord Street Bridge	Across Whitechapel between Lord Street and Church Street (OS:SJ34559029).	Remains of stone abutments and part of an arch were uncovered during building excavations in that area in 1805 (120).
34. Fall Well	Queen Square/St John's Lane, close to the junction with Roe Street (OS:SJ34869057).	The well is not shown on Charles Eyes' plan of 1785. In 1778 the Corporation was to discuss its future as the walls had been knocked down and the site was dangerous. When the well was no longer used by the public, the water was piped to the garden of a house occupied by Sir William Roe at the north end of Queen Square, where it formed a fountain (121).

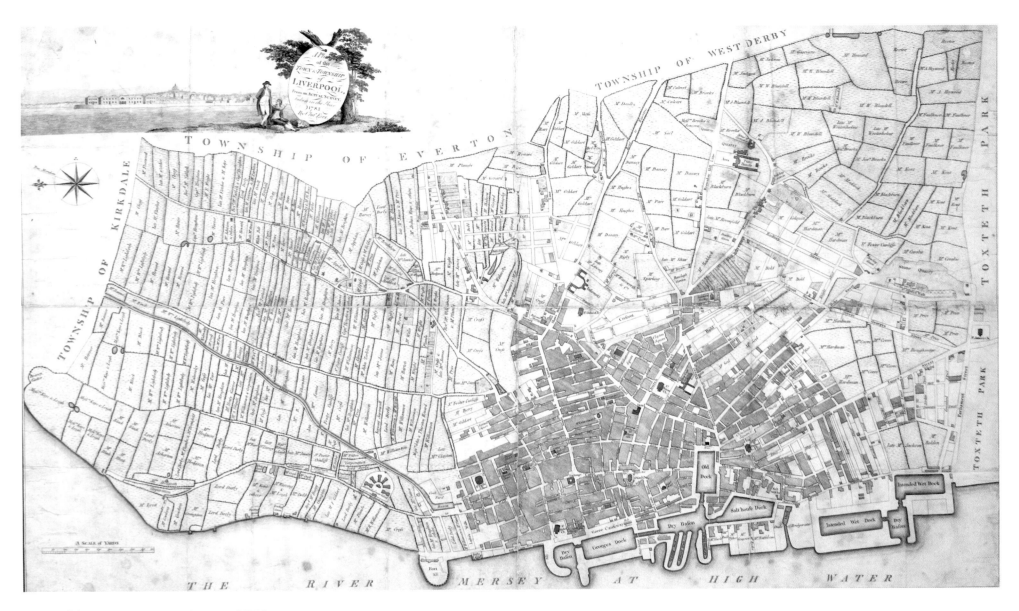

Figure 34: *Charles Eyes' plan of Liverpool 1785.*

Front cover clockwise from left:
Section of John Eyes' plan of Liverpool dated 1765 showing Liverpool Infirmary , the Old Dock and the triangle of roads formed by Paradise Street, Church Street and Hanover Street.
Detail of Liverpool Castle from a view of Liverpool about 1680.
'The South West Prospect of Liverpool ...' 1728 by S and N Buck.
Excavation in progress on Brownlow Hill at the site of William Reid's China factory 1997-98.

Back cover:
View of Liverpool as it was around 1680 showing St Nicholas' Church, the Tower and the Castle adjacent to the river. The Town Hall appears in the middle ground.

Acknowledgements:

All the figures have been provided and reproduced by courtesy of Liverpool Record Office, at Liverpool Central Library, William Brown Street, Liverpool except for the following:

Figures 6, 7, 13 (St Paul's inset) courtesy of Merseyside Archaeological Service.
Figures 10, 33 (main picture and excavation inset), front cover (Brownlow Hill excavation) courtesy of National Museums Liverpool, Field Archaeology Section.
Figures 2, 4, 8, 14 (inset), 19, 21, 24, 29, 32 by Dave Roberts, Merseyside Archaeological Society.

Other maps referred to in the text but not listed above (all available in Liverpool Record Office):
1796 A plan of the Town of Liverpool by John Gore.
1803 Plan of the Township of Liverpool by R. Horwood.
1816 Plan of Liverpool by Thomas Kaye.
1821 A plan of the Township of Liverpool by W. S. Sherwood.
1835 Map of the Town and Port of Liverpool by Michael Alexander Gage.
1849 Plan of the Borough of Liverpool by James Newlands.

Notes and Bibliography

Abbreviations

JMAS: Journal of Merseyside Archaeological Society.
Liverpool RO: Liverpool Record Office.
LWHSG: Liverpool World Heritage Steering Group
NML: National Museums Liverpool.
OAN: Oxford Archaeology North.
OS: Ordnance Survey: copies of records held in SMR.
PPS: Proceedings of the Prehistoric Society.
SMR: Merseyside Sites and Monuments Record.
Rec Soc Lancs Ches: Record Society of Lancashire and Cheshire.
THSLC : Transactions of the Historic Society of Lancashire and Cheshire.
TLCAS: Transactions of the Lancashire and Cheshire Antiquarian Society.

Notes

Topography

1. Stewart-Brown 1932.
2. Hewitt 1886.
3. Twemlow 1935, 22, 518; Chandler and Wilson 1965, 128.
4. Hewitt 1886, 147.
5. Godwin 1959.
6. Davey 1977, 13.
7. Twemlow 1918, 9.
8. Brownbill and Walker 1913, 2.
9. Stewart-Brown 1932, 88.

Liverpool before 1207

1. Forde-Johnston 1957.
2. Chitty 1977.
3. Cowell, 1995, JMAS 9, 25-44.
4. Cowell and Philpott, 2000.
5. Smith, H. E., 1870, 267.
6. OS Record Card SJ 39 SWI.
7. OS Record Card SJ 39 SEI8.
8. Gladstone 1932, 8.
9. Philpott, forthcoming, JMAS 12.
10. Harrison 1892, 250.
11. Edwards, forthcoming, JMAS 12.
12. Philpott, forthcoming, JMAS 12.
13. Farrer 1902, 432-3.

Historical Overview

Municipal and lordship
1. Philpott 1991, 105-120.
2. Kermode et al 2006, 59-112.
3. Baines 1870, 350.
4. Pamphlet for Free Borough on the Sea Exhibition at Liverpool Central Library. February-June 2007.

5. Port Cities web site.
6. Kermode et al 2006, 99.
7. Brooke 1853, 216-7.
8. Stewart-Brown 1917, 24-72.

Commerce and Trade
1. Kermode et al 2006, 59-112.
2. Longmore 2006, 113-170.
3. Muir 1911, 1-57.

The Docks
1. Quartermaine web site 2007.
2. Picton 1875, 556.
3. Richie-Noakes 1984, 19.
4. Richie-Noakes 1984, 23.
5. Richie-Noakes 1984, 27.

Markets
1. Brooke 1853 chapter 2.

Fairs
1. Chandler and Wilson 1965, 75.
2. Brooke 1853, 222.
3. Stonehouse 1869, 102.

Industries
Mills and Milling
1. Moss 1796 (1974), 113.
2. Bennett and Elton 1904, 125-26.
3. Bennet and Elton 1904, 180-81.
4. Enfield 1773, 89.

Salt
1. Stonehouse 1869, 183.

Sugar Refining
1. LWHSG 2003, 108; Chandler 1957, 332.
2. King 2000.

Tanning
1. Belcham 2006, 74.

Pottery
1. Davey BAR BS78, 124-127.
2. Liverpool Museum website.
3. Picton 1873, 340-344 and 545; Jeff Speakman (pers. comm.).

Glass Manufacture
1. Hurst-Vose forthcoming, JMAS 13.

Silk Manufacture
1. Hertz 1909, 710.

Brewing and Distilling
1. Barge 1987, 1.
2. Shaw & Shaw 1907, 5.
3. Enfield 1773, 88.

Rope Manufacture
1. Irvine 1899.

Places of Worship and Crosses
1. Touzeau 1910, 387.
2. Brooke 1853, 49-58.

Charitable Institutions
Schools
1. Farrer and Brownbill 1908, 593-5.
2. Chandler and Saxton 1960, 99.
3. Farrer and Brownbill 1966, 10.
4. Touzeau 1910, 406-9.
5. Picton 1873, 195.
6. Picton 1873, 196.
7. Enfield 1773, 48-9.
8. Young 1913, 94.
9. Touzeau 1910, 409-10.
10. Longmore 2006, 162.
11. Shaw and Shaw 1907, 30, 40.
12. Picton 1873, 2, 129, 226.
13. Farrer and Brownbill 1911, 54-5.
14. Young 1913, 94.
15. Longmore 2006, 144-6.
16. Chandler 1957, 101.
17. Royden 1991, 264.
18. Farrer and Brownbill 1911, 53.

Almshouses and Workhouses
1. Young 1913, 84.
2. Picton 1873, 60.
3. Irvine 1899, 43.
4. Young 1913, 84.
5. Twemlow 1918, 104, 752.
6. Irvine 1899, 16, 33.
7. Picton 1873, 2, 146.
8. Picton 1883, 318.
9. Chandler 1957, 258.
10. Young 1913, 62.
11. Farrer and Brownbill 1911, 55.
12. Peet 1912, 1-4.
13. Enfield 1773.
14. Higginbotham 2006, 54-56.
15. McLoughlin 1978, 11-28.
16. Enfield 1773, 55.

Law and Order
1. Chandler and Saxton 1960, 52.
2. Ascot, Lewis and Power 2006, 146.

Medieval 1207-1539 Chapter

1. Farrer and Brownbill 1911 , 2.
2. Chandler 1957, 220-1.
3. Chandler 1957, 13-41.
4. Brownbill and Walker 1913; Lumby 1939; Radcliffe 1890, 1892, 1893, 1894.
5. Twemlow 1935, 894.
6. Twemlow 1918, 15-16.
7. Brownbill and Walker 1913, 38.
8. Chandler and Wilson 1965, 145.
9. Stewart-Brown 1925, 69-70.
10. Muir and Platt 1906, 296.
11. Brownbill and Walker 1913.
12. Stewart-Brown 1917, 2.
13. Stewart-Brown 1917, 52-3.
14. Stewart-Brown 1917, 69-72.
15. Kermode et al, 2006, 69.

Medieval 1207-1539 Gazetteer

1. Chandler 1957, 20-1.
2. Cox 1892, 193.
3. Farrer 1915, 68.
4. Troughton 1810, 47.
5. Cox 1892, 196; Larkin 1928, 186-7, Fig. 3.
6. Farrer and Brownbill 1911, 6.
7. Picton 1883, 9; Cox 1892, 203.
8. Farrer and Brownbill 1911 , 6.
9. Picton 1873, 4-5; Fishwick 1902, 19, 61-3.
10. Cox 1892, 205.
11. Picton 1873, 2, 37.
12. Peet 1908, 71; Stewart-Brown 1912, 105; Picton 1873, 2, 37.
13. Stewart-Brown 1910, 82.
14. Picton 1873, 2, 80.
15. Bailey 1949, 38-41.
16. Brownbill and Walker 1913, 84.
17. Farrer and Brownbill 1911, 10n, 147.
18. Elton 1904, 78-9, 85.
19. Twemlow 1935, 1043.
20. Peet 1915, 497.
21. Farrer and Brownbill 1908, 593-5.
22. Elton 1904, 79-80, 82.
23. Peet 1908, 102.
24. Elton 1904, 85.
25. Brownbill and Walker 1913, 74.
26. Irvine 1899, 43.
27. Twemlow 1935, 1030.
28. Farrer and Brownbill 1911 , 9.
29. Bennett and Elton 1904, 128.
30. Farrer and Brownbill 1911 , 9; Bennett and Elton 1904, 128-36.
31. Bennett and Elton 1904, 136-43; Farrer and Brownbill 1911, 9.
32. Bennett and Elton 1904, 142.
33. Bennett and Elton 1904, 175; Farrer and Brownbill 1908, 275; Farrer and Brownbill 1911, 9.

34. Brownbill and Walker 1913, 90.
35. Bennett and Elton 1904, 176.
36. Bennett and Elton 1904, 154-7; 142.
37. Muir and Platt 1906, 316.
38. Bennett and Elton 1904, 175-6, 161-6.
39. Lumby 1939, 195.
40. Brownbill and Walker 1913, 28, 96.
41. Brownbill and Walker 1913, 33, 34.
42. Lumby 1939, 195.
43. Brownbill and Walker 1913, 96; Stewart-Brown 1917, 48.
44. Brownbill and Walker 1913, 34, 85.
45. Radcliffe 1893, 344.
46. Taylor, 1902, 191.
47. NML note from Geology Department ; OS Record Card: SJ 39 SW 24; LWHSG 2003, p 105.
48. OS Record Card: SJ 39 SW 25.

Tudor, Early Stuart and Commonwealth 1540-1659 Chapter
1. Peet 1909, xii-xiii.
2. Twemlow 1935, 22.
3. Chandler and Wilson, 1965, 128.
4. Twemlow 1918, Twemlow 1935; Chandler and Saxton 1960; Chandler and Wilson 1965.
5. Twemlow 1935, 2.
6 Twemlow 1918, Twemlow 1935.
7. Twemlow 1935, 659-60.
8. Twemlow 1935, 175.
9. Twemlow 1935, 308; Chandler and Wilson 1965, 222.
10. Farrer and Brownbill 1911, 20; Chandler and Wilson 1965, 353.
11. Chandler 1957, 48.
12. Stonehouse 1852, 72.
13. Davey 1977, 14; McNeil, 1985, 30f.
14. Picton 1883, 140, 189.
15. Chandler and Wilson 1965, 363, 31.
16. LWHSG 2003, 121.
17. LWHSG 2003, 108f.
18. Kermode et al 2006, 76.

Tudor, Early Stuart and Commonwealth 1540-1659 Gazetteer
1. Gladstone 1908.
2. Chandler and Wilson 1965, 405.
3. Picton 1883, 189.
4. Stonor 1957, 25.
5. Chandler 1957, 135-6; Liverpool RO 920 MOO no. 272.
6. Stewart-Brown 1910, 46.
7. Stewart-Brown 1910, 47.
8. Bailey 1949, 38-41.
9. Twemlow 1935, 25.
10. Elton 1904,93-8.
11. Elton 1904, 117; Twemlow 1935, 1044-5.
12. Peet 1915, 497-9; Chandler and Saxton 1960, 149.
13. Twemlow 1918, 1935; Chandler and Wilson 1965, 37;

Chandler and Saxton 1960, 154; Picton 1883, 213.
14. Chandler and Saxton 1960, 268.
15. Chandler and Wilson 1965, 140, 208.
16. Troughton 1810, 63.
17. Irvine 1899, 43.
18. Twemlow 1935, 1030; Chandler and Wilson 1965.
19. Bennett and Elton 1904, 143, 148-52; Twemlow 1918, 422; Chandler and Saxton 1960, 274; Chandler and Wilson 1965, 135, 172.
20. Bennett and Elton 1904, 152, 153, 150.
21. Bennett and Elton 1904, 176.
22. Twemlow 1918, 1935; Chandler and Saxton 1960; Chandler and Wilson 1965.
23. Chandler and Wilson 1965, 145.
24. Bennett and Elton 1904, 150, 157-9; 160-8.
25. Bennett and Elton 1904, 164-5.
26. Radcliffe 1894, 226.
27. Chandler and Wilson 1965, 202.
28. Irvine, 1899.
29. Picton 1873, 60; Twemlow 1918, 104 n 6.
30. Irvine, 1899, 752.
31. Twemlow 1918, 265, 150.
32. Twemlow 1918, Twemlow 1935; Chandler and Wilson 1965.
33. Chandler and Wilson 1965, 347.
34. Twemlow 1935, 175, 181, 183.
35. Twemlow 1935, 308; Chandler and Wilson 1965, 222; Picton 1883, 229.
36. Twemlow 1918, 123-4.
37. Twemlow 1935, 223.
38. Chandler and Wilson 1965, 189.
39. Elton 1904, 108, n.7O.
40. Twemlow 1918, 21; Twemlow 1935, 7; Chandler and Wilson 1965, 127, 157.
41. Picton 1883, 192; Chandler and Saxton, 1960, 75.
42. Twemlow 1918, 123-4.
43. Picton 1883, 192.
44. Twemlow 1918, 249, 562, 576; Chandler and Wilson 1965; 189.
45. Chandler and Saxton 1960, 202, 386; Picton 1883, 188.
46. Twemlow 1918, 399; Twemlow 1935, 459; Chandler and Saxton 1960, 181, 185; Chandler and Wilson 1965, 185, 199, 202.

Later Stuart 1660-1713 Chapter
1. Irvine 1899, 167-70.
2. Peet 1908, 59.
3. Irvine 1899.
4. Peet 1908.
5. Peet 1908, 27 n. I.
6. Irvine 1899, 35, 94.
7. Peet 1908, 41.
8. Peet 1908, 29-32.

9. Stewart-Brown 1917, 65-6.
10. Picton 1883, 275-8.
11. Peet 1908, 32, 102.
12. Stewart-Brown 1932, 92; LWHSG 2003, 121.
13. Farrer and Brownbill 1911, 22-3, 17.
14. Picton 1886, 48-9; Chandler 1957, 55, 292.
15. Peet 1909, xii-xiii.
16. Chandler 1957, 332.
17. Chandler and Wilson 1965, 310, 325; Peet 1910, 154.
18. Tyrer 1968, 261.
19. Peet 1909, 140, 141.
20. Bennett and Elton 1904, 180.
21. Peet 1908, 50, 95.
22. Tyrer 1970, 113.
23. Picton 1883, 285; Picton 1886, 84.
24. Kermode et al, 2006, 108, 169.
25. Tyrer 1970, 113.
26. Kermode et al 2006, 108; Longmore 2006, 169.

Later Stuart (1660-1713) Gazetteer
1. Peet 1912, 409, 426; Picton 1883, 292.
2. Peet 1908, 87n.; Peet 1912, 418n.I, 420, 422.
3. Peet1908, 94-5; Peet 1909, xii-xiii.
4. Larkin 1928.
5. Picton 1886, 42-3; Touzeau 1910, 384.
6. Tyrer 1968, 217.
7. Tyrer 1970, 23, 113.
8. Picton 1903, 2, 33-4.
9. Peet 1908, 71; Farrer and Brownbill 1911, 24.
10. Stewart-Brown 1910, 49-51.
11. Peet 1908, 55.
12. Stewart-Brown 1910,47.
13. Touzeau 1910, 291.
14. Picton 1883, 270-1, 286.
15. Twemlow 1935, 1048.
16. Peet 1908, 110.3; Gladstone 1932; 19-21.
17. Radcliffe 1894, 230.
18. Gladstone 1932, 19-21; Picton 1883,270-1.
19. Gladstone 1932, 19-21.
20. Peet 1912,I; Peet 1915; Peet 1908, 103.
21. Peet 1912, 426; Picton 1873, 2, 173-75.
22. Picton 1883, 2, 330-31.
23. Peet 1908, 42, 100-01n.
24. Peet 1908, 65n.
25. Peet 1908, 76; Murphy 1955, 87,90.
26. Stonor 1957, 26-7; Peet 1908, 34, 40, 91, 107-108.
27. Peet 1908, 118.
28. Irvine 1899,43.
29. Twemlow 1935, 1030; Touzeau 1910, 290.
30. Twemlow 1918, 416; Twemlow 1935, 1028-9.
31. Peet 1908, 72,73.
32. Twemlow 1935, 1048.
33. Chandler 1957, 274; Peet 1908, 27.
34. Peet 1908, 56.
35. Ritchie-Noakes 1984, 19, 22.
36. Tyrer 1968, 261.

37. SMR field notes; Quartermaine web site 2007.
38. Ritchie-Noakes 1984, 19; Picton 1886; Touzeau 1910, 1. 74.
39. Bennett and Elton 1904, 169.
40. Picton 1883, 342; Bennett and Elton 1904, 180.
41. Peet 1908, 50, 113.
42. Irvine 1899, 63-7.
43. Peet 1908, 55, 83.
44. Peet 1908, 118, 117.
45. Irvine 1899, 87.
46. Picton 1883, 342; Bennett and Elton 1904, 180.
47. Peet 1908, 50, 115.
48. Bennett and Elton 1904, 177; Irvine 1899, 68.
49. Peet 1908, 23, 84.
50. Peet 1908, 60; Irvine 1899, 65; Bennett and Elton 1904, 153.
51. Peet 1908, 50, 78.
52. Peet 1908, 47, 117.
53. Peet 1908, 50, 109, 114.
54. Peet 1908, 116.
55. Brownbill and Walker 1913, 59.
56. Peet 1908, 62-3.
57. Barker, 1951.
58. Peet 1908, 37, 95.
59. Chandler 1957, 332; Peet 1908, 32, 91.
60. Peet 1908, 40, 108.
61. Peet 1908, 43, 101.
62. Peet 1908, 37, 116.
63. Peet 1908, 78.
64. Peet 1908, 100.
65. Gatty 1881, 126; Peet 1908, 95.
66. Brooke, 1853, 151.
67. Touzeau 1910, I 272.
68. Aughton 1990, 217.
69. Touzeau, 1910, I 323.
70. Irvine 1899, 16, 33, 43, 60.
71. Picton 1883, 318; Peet 1912, 3-4; Farrer and Brownbill 1911, 55.
72. Peet 1912, 1-4, 389.
73. Picton 1886, 45; Peet 1912, 385; Peet 1912(a), 3.
74. Peet 1908, 28, 148; Peet 1912, 4; Peet 1915, 385; Farrer and Brownbill 1911, 55.
75. Chandler 1957, 384.
76. Picton 1873, 195; Twemlow 1935, 1047; Touzeau 1910, 406-09; Chandler 1957, 384.
77. Peet 1908, 112, 115.
78. Touzeau 1910, 301.
79. Irvine 1899, 33; Picton 1883, 338; Picton 1886, 81.
80. Tyrer 1968, 91.
81. Tyrer 1968, 295.
82. Touzeau 1910, 301.
83. Picton 1883, 318.
84. Picton 1883, 294; Brooke, 1853, 114.
85. Picton 1883, 315.
86. Stewart-Brown 1932, plan 2.
87. Picton 1883, 188.
88. Stewart-Brown 1932, 126 and plan 2.

89. Irvine 1899, 141.
90. Picton 1883, 275-6, 278; Twemlow 1935, 257.
91. Stewart-Brown 1932, plan 2.
92. Brooke 1853, 127-8.
93. Irvine 1899, 124-6; 132 Picton 1883, 320.

George I - George III 1714-1770 Chapter

1. McNeil R and Newman R, 2006, 154f.
2. Picton 1886.
3. Stewart-Brown 1917, 61-6.
4. Stewart-Brown 1917, 66.
5. Bagley, 1956, 40.
6. Farrer and Brownbill 1911, 30; Longmore, 2006, 12.
7. Longmore 2006, 10, citing Ascott, Lewis and Power.
8. Enfield 1773 67.
9. Longmore 2006 4.
10. Longmore 2006, 169.

George I - George III 1714-1770 Gazetteer

Municipal and lordship
1. Peet 1912, 426; Picton 1886, 42.
2. Picton 1886, 61.
3. Chandler 1957, 151.
4. Picton 1873, 2, 38.
5. Picton 1873, 2, 91-2.
6. Stewart-Brown 1910, 60-81.
7. Twemlow 1935, 1049.
8. Radcliffe 1894, 231.
9. Peet 1908, 110.
10. Picton 1886, 157; Young and Young 1913.
11. Chandler 1957, 202, 213.
12. McLoughlin 1978.
13. Picton 1875, 91.
14. Visitors Guide to Liverpool. 1886 9-10.
15. Brooke 1853.

Places of worship
16. Peet 1915, 500.
17. Jackson 1968, plate 10.
18. Peet 1915, 500-01.
19. Peet 1908, 102-03.
20. Peet 1912, Peet 1915.
21. Chandler 1957, 455; Peet 1908, 143; Lewis, 2001.
22. Farrer and Brownbill 1911; Peet 1908 100.
23. Farrer and Brownbill 1911, 47, 50; Lewis, 2001 19.
24. Farrer and Brownbill 1911, 50; Murphy 1955, 95, 98.
25. Stonor 1957, 27-8, 31-2; Farrer and Brownbill 1911, 51; Lewis, 2001 17f.
26. Peet 1912, 426.
27. Farrer and Brownbill 1911, 46; Enfield 1773 44; Sharples 2004, 179.
28. Peet 1901, 30; Jackson 1968, plate 13 and text opposite; Lewis, 2001, 11.

29. Enfield 1773, 47; Picton 1873, 2, 107-08.
30. Peet 1908, 118; Farrer and Brownbill 1911, 49, 33; Lewis, 2001, 14.
31. Enfield 1773, 44-45, Lewis 2001, 23.
32. Farrer and Brownbill 1911; Enfield 1773,47; Brooke 1853, 58; Lewis 2001, 10.
33. Farrer and Brownbill 1911, 4, 49; Brooke 1853, 58.
34. Picton 1875, 175; Brooke 1853, 60f.
35. Picton 1875, II, 187; Peet 1901, 39; Hand 1907, 111.
36. Farrer and Brownbill 1911; Enfield 1773, 45f; Lewis 2001, 20.
37. OAN, 2005, and 2006, unpubl.
38. Farrer and Brownbill 1911; Lewis 2001, 24.

Commerce
39. Young 1913, 79.
40. Rideout 1928, 5.
41. Picton 1873, 2, 92-3.
42. Picton 1886, 63; Rideout 1928, 5: Sharples 2004,178.
43. Picton 1886, 377.

Docks
44. Tyrer 1970, 145.
45. Picton 1886, 50-1.
46. Ritchie-Noakes 1984, 19.
47. Ritchie-Noakes 1984, 19.
48. Picton 1886, 50.
49. Picton 1875, 156.
50. Ritchie-Noakes 1984, 19, 21-2.
51. Ritchie-Noakes 1984, 23.
52. Picton 1875, 557.
53. Ritchie-Noakes 1984, 19; Harris 1939.
54. Ritchie-Noakes 1984, 19.
55. Ritchie-Noakes 1984, 27-8.
56. Ritchie-Noakes 1984, 27-8.
57. Ritchie-Noakes 1984, 27-8.

Industrial
Mills
58. Bennett and Elton 1904, 182-3, fig. p. 124.
59. Bennett and Elton 1904, 164n.
60. Bennett and Elton 1904 198-89.
61. Bennett and Elton 1904 198-89.
62. Bennett and Elton 1904 198-89.
63. Bennett and Elton 1904 198-89.
64. Bennett and Elton 1904 134, 198-89, 203.
65. Jeff Speakman (pers. comm.)
66. Bennett and Elton 1904 198-89, 203-06.
67. Bennett and Elton 1904 198-89, 206.
68. Picton 1873, II 293.

Salt
69. Barker 1951.

Sugar
70. Mawer 2007; Wardle 1946, SMR reference.

Pot Works
71. Walker Art Gallery, Decorative Arts Records.
72. Gatty 1881, 127, 137.
73. Gatty 1881, 135, 136.
74. Picton 1873, 113, 342.
75. Gatty 1881, 124; Mayer 1854, p 189.
76. Gatty 1881, p 134.
77. Gatty 1881, p 134.
78. Philpott 2004.

Glass works
79. Tyrer 1972, 121.
80. Gatty 1881, 127; Buckley 1925; Harris 2001.
81. Buckley 1925; Picton, 1873, II, p 336; Harris, 2001.
82. Hurst Vose, forthcoming, JMAS 12; Buckley 1925.

Silk
83. Chandler, 1957, p 332; Picton, 1873, 75.

Ropewalks
84. Touzeau 1910 II, 531; Brooke 1853 146.
85. Aughton, 1990, 221.
86. McLoughlin, 1978, 49.
87. Aughton, 1990, 216.

Other Buildings
88. Peet 1913, 180, 182, 231; Brooke 1853, 79.
89. Brooke 1853, 135; Stonehouse 1869, 156.
90. Bailey 1946.
91. SMR paper record.
92. Picton 1875, p. 293; Longmore, 2006, 13.
93. Picton 1875, p. 293.
94. Picton 1875, p. 135.
95. Picton 1875, 42; Moss W 1796.
96. Picton 1875, 43.
97. SMR sheets.
98. Picton 1875, II, 206: Picton 1853, 112.
99. Brooke 1853, 89-91: Baines 1870, 369; Royden 1991, 23.

Charity
100. Picton 1873 II, 146.
101. Chandler 1957, 391; Baines 1870, 355; Enfield 1773, 56.
102. Peet 1912, 1-4; Picton,1886, 155-6.
103. Peet 1908, 28-9; Chandler 1957, 258; Liverpool RO Binns Coll 10.86.4ff; Parrott 2005, 102.
104. Peet 1908, 93n.
105. Peet 1908, 93n, 149-50; Peet 1912, 3; Picton 1886, 63; Touzeau 1910, 436-37.
106. Farrer and Brownbill 1908, 2, 595; Touzeau 1910, 409-11; Baines 1870, 372.

107. Touzeau 1910, 406-09; Twemlow 1935, 1046; Chandler 1957, 384-5; Peet 1908, 90.
108. Picton 1873 II, 129.

Law and Order
109. Stonehouse, 1869, 30.
110. Picton 1886, 81.
111. Davey, 1985, 16f; Picton 1873, 2, 13.
112. Picton 1886, 130; Picton 1873, 2, 13; Brooke, 1853, 528.
113. Davey 1985, 17.
114. Davey, 1985, 14f and fig 4c.

Crosses
115. Picton 1886, 257, 259.
116. Picton 1886, 155; Peet 1915, 402-03; Taylor 1902, 192.
117. Cox 1898, 179.
118. Hand, 1907, 67.

Bridges
119. Picton 1903, 2, 89.
120. Brooke 1853, 127-8.
121. Picton 1886, 273; Picton 1873, 2, 194.

Bibliography
Ascott D., Lewis F. and Power M. 2006 *Liverpool 1660-1750*.
Aughton P. 1990 *Liverpool, A People's History*.

Bagley J.J. 1956 *A History of Lancashire*.
Bagley J.J. 1957 'Eight lines of Latin started a city', *Lancashire Life* 5 *6 (June)* 33-35. Manchester.
Bailey F.A. 1949 'Some Memoranda by William Moore Esq., concerning Liverpool and Walton 1510-1512' *THSLC* **100**, 33-44.
Bailey 1946 SMR reference.
Baines E. 1868 *A History of the County Palatine and Duchy of Lancaster* **1**.
Baines E. 1870 *A History of the County Palatine and Duchy of Lancaster* **2**.
Barge J. 1987 *A Gazetteer of Liverpool's Breweries*.
Barker T.C. 1951 'Lancashire Coal, Cheshire Salt, and the Rise of Liverpool', *THSLC* **103**.
Belchem J. (ed.) 2006 *Liverpool 800 Culture Character and History* Liverpool University Press.
Bennet R. and Elton J. 1904 *Some Feudal Mills History of Corn Milling* **4**, London and Liverpool.
Brooke R. 1853 *Liverpool as it was during the last quarter of the eighteenth century, 1755-1800*. Liverpool.
Brownbill J. and Walker K. 1913 'Calendar of Deeds and Papers of the Moore Family of Bankhall', *Rec Soc Lancs Ches* **67**.
Buckley F. 1925 *A History of Old English Glass*. Ernest Benn Limited, London.

Chandler G. 1957 *Liverpool*. London.
Chandler G. 1972 *An Illustrated History of Liverpool*. Rondo Publications, Liverpool.
Chandler G. and Saxton E.B. 1960 *Liverpool Under James I*. Liverpool.
Chandler G. and Wilson E.K. 1965 *Liverpool Under Charles1*. Liverpool.
Chitty G. 1977 'Excavations at Wavertree, March 1976' *JMAS* **1**, 11-12.
Connelly P. A. and Philpott R. 1998 An Archaeological Trial Excavation at Nos 36-58 Brownlow Hill (unpublished).
Cowell R.W. 1995 'Some Neolithic and Bronze Age Finds from Merseyside and the North West' *JMAS* **9**, 25-44.
Cowell R.W. and Philpott R.A. 2000 *Prehistoric, Romano-British and Mediaeval Settlement in Lowland North West England*.
Cox C. 2001 Archaeological Desk-based Assessment : Site of the former St Paul's Eye Hospital, Old Hall Street. (unpublished).
Cox E.W. 1892 'An Attempt to Recover the Plans of the Castle of Liverpool from authentic records',*THSLC* **42** n.s.**6**, 195-254.
Cox E.W. 1898 'Leaves from an Antiquary's Note Book', *THSLC* **49** n.s. **13**, 178-184.
Criminal punishments at the Old Bailey late 17th to early 19th century www.oldbaileyonline.org/history/crime/punishment.html (2007)
Crosby A. (ed.) 1998 *Leading the Way. A History of Lancashire's Roads*.

Davey P.J. 1977 'South Castle Street 1976: Interim Report' *JMAS* **1**, 13-16.
Davey P.J. 1980 'The Archaeology of the Clay Tobacco Pipe III Britain: The North and West'. *BAR British Series* **78**.
Davey P.J. 1985 'Excavations in South Castle Street: The 1976 Excavations' *JMAS* **4**, 6-19.

Edwards B. 'Merseyside in the Dark Ages' *JMAS* **12** (forthcoming).
Elton J. 1904 'The Chapel of St Mary del Key, Liverpool' *THSLC* **54** n.s. **18**, 73-118.
Enfield W. 1773 *An Essay towards the History of Liverpool*. Warrington.

Farrer W. 1902 *The Lancashire Pipe Rolls (1130-1216) ...and early Lancashire Charters...from..William Rufus to King John*. Liverpool.

Farrer W. (ed) 1915 'Lancashire Inquests, Extents and Feudal Aids 3, 1313-1355', *Rec Soc Lancs Ches* **70**.
Farrer W. and Brownbill J. 1907 *Victoria County history of the Counties of England: A History of the County of Lancaster* **3**. Archibald Constable and Co., London.
Farrer W. and Brownbill J. 1908 *Victoria County history of the Counties of England: A History of the County of Lancaster* **2**. Archibald Constable and Co., London.
Farrer W. and Brownbill J. 1911 *Victoria County history of the Counties of England: A History of the County of Lancaster* **4**. Archibald Constable and Co., London.
Fishwick H. 1902 'The Old Castles of Liverpool' *TLCAS* **19**, 45-76
Forde-Johnston J. L. 1957 'Megalithic Art in the North-west of Britain: the Calderstones, Liverpool', *PPS* **23**, 20-39.

Gatty C. 1881 'The Liverpool Potteries' *THSLC* **33**, 123-168.
Gifford 2006 An Archaeological Survey of Canning Dock Wall (unpublished).
Gladstone R. 1908 'A Report on Liverpool Castle 2nd October 1559', *THSLC* **59** n.s. **23**, 162-164.
Gladstone R. 1932 *Notes on the History and Antiquities of Liverpool*. Liverpool.
Godwin H. 1959 'Studies of the postglacial history of British vegetation. XIV. Late Glacial deposits at Moss Lake, Liverpool', *Phil Trans Roy Soc London*.

Hand C.R. 1907 *Olde Liverpoole and its Charter*.
Harris A. 2002 A Study of Historic Development: Buildings at 91-95 Old Hall Street (unpublished).
Harris S.A. 1939 *THSLC* **89**, **91**.
Harris E.C. 2001 City Square: Liverpool Archaeological Desk Top Study Report.(unpublished).
Harrison W. 1893 'Archaeological finds in Lancashire', *TLCAS* **10**, 249-252.
Hertz G.B. 1909 'The English Silk Industry in the Eighteenth Century', *English Historical Review*, **XXIV (XCVI)**, 710.
Hewitt W. 1886 'Notes on the Topography of Liverpool', *Proceedings of the Geological Society* **5** part **2**, 145-154.
Higginbotham P. 2006 *Workhouses of the North*. Tempus.
Horn D.B. and Ransome M. (eds.) *English Historical Documents 1714-1783*. Hodder & Stoughton.
Hughes J. 1906 *Liverpool Banks and Bankers, 1760-1837*.
Hurst Vose R. 'The Glass Industry in Merseyside and its environs 1500-1750' *JMAS* **12** (forthcoming).

Irvine W.F. 1899 *Liverpool in King Charles the Second's Time*. Liverpool.

Jackson W.C.M. 1968 *Herdman's Liverpool*. Liverpool.

Kermode J., Hollinshead J. and Gratton M. 2006 'Small Beginnings: Liverpool 1207-1680' in Belchem J. (ed.) *Liverpool 800*. 59-112.
King N. 2000 Article at http://www.mawer.clara.net/liverpool.html
Knoop D. 2003 Article at http://www.mawer.clara.net/liverpool.html

Larkin F.C. 1928 'Excavations on the site of Liverpool Castle', *THSLC* **79** 179-197.
Lea J.L. 2004 *Ideology and the Gallows in 18th and 19th century England*.
Lewis D. 2001 *The Churches of Liverpool*.
Liverpool Museum web-site. NML 2007 Brownlow Hill, Liverpool, the site of William Reid's porcelain factory. http://www.liverpool museums.org.uk/mol/archaeology/fieldarchaeology/postmedbrownlow.asp
Liverpool World Heritage Steering Group 2003 *Liverpool Maritime Mercantile City (Liverpool World Heritage) Liverpool*. Liverpool University Press.
Longmore J. 'Cemented by the Blood of a Negro?' The Impact of the Slave Trade on Liverpool, a paper presented at the Liverpool and transatlantic Slavery Conference on 15 October 2005.

Longmore J. 2006 'Civic Liverpool: 1680-1800' in Belcham J. (ed.) *Liverpool 800*. 113-170.
Lumby J.H. 1939 'A calendar of the Norris Deeds (Lancashire) 12th to 15th Century', *Rec Soc Lancs Ches* **93**.
Matrix Archaeology, 2001 Cleveland Square, Liverpool City Centre Archaeological Assessment (unpublished).
Mawer B. Sugar Website (2007) http://www.mawer.clara.net/liverpool.html
Mayer 1854 SMR reference
McLoughlin G. 1978 *A Short History of the First Liverpool Infirmary 1749-1821*. Phillimore.
McNeil R. 1985 'Excavations in South Castle Street: The 1977 excavations' *JMAS* **4**, 20-32.
McNeil R. and Newman R. 2006 The Archaeology of North West England, An Archaeological Research Framework for North West England **1** Resource Assessment.
Merseyside Archaeological Society 1982 *The Calderstones: A prehistoric tomb in Liverpool*.
Moss 1796 (1974) *The Liverpool Guide*. Liverpool.
Muir R. and Platt E.M. 1906 *A History of Municipal Government in Liverpool*. London.
Muir R. 1911 'West Derby Hundred - Liverpool' Farrer W. and Brownbill J. (eds.) 1911 *The Victoria History of the Counties of England: A History of Lancashire* **4**. Archibald Constable and Co., London. 1-57.
Murphy J. 1955 'The Old Quaker Meeting House in Hackins Hey, Liverpool', *THSLC* **106**, 79-98.

Oxford Archaeology North, 2006, Mann Island, Liverpool. Archaeological Evaluation Report (unpublished).
Oxford Archaeology North, 2006 St Paul's Square, Liverpool. Archaeological Watching Brief (unpublished).
Oxford Archaeology North, 2006, Liverpool Canal Link. Archaeological Evaluation (unpublished).
Oxford Archaeology North, 2005, Land at St Paul's Square, Liverpool. Archaeological Evaluation (unpublished).
Oxford Archaeology North, 2005, Canning Dock Watching Brief and Evaluation (unpublished).
Oxford Archaeology North, 2005, Canning Dock Liverpool, Phase 2, Archaeological Evaluation (unpublished).

Parrott K. 2005 *Pictorial Liverpool: The Art of WG and William Herdman*. Liverpool.
Peet H. 1901 'Brief historical notes on the churches of St. George and St. John , Liverpool' *THSLC* **51** n.s. **15**, 27-44.
Peet H. 1908 'Liverpool in the Reign of Queen Anne 1705 and 1708' *THSLC* **59** n.s. **23**, Appendix I - 177.
Peet H. (ed.) 1909 'The Earliest Registers of the Parish of Liverpool …1604 to 1704. With some of the earlier Episcopal Transcripts commencing in 1604', *Lancashire Parish Register Society* **35.**
Peet H. (ed.) 1912 *Liverpool Vestry Books: 1 1681-1799*. Liverpool and London.
Peet H. 1912(a) 'Liverpool Almshouses', *THSLC* **63** n.s. **27**, 1-4.
Peet H. 1915 *Liverpool Vestry Books: 2 1800-1834. With supplementary extracts 1835-1842*. Liverpool and London.
Philpott R.A. 1991 'Medieval Towns' *JMAS* **7**, 105-120.
Philpott R.A. 2004 Summary of Archaeological Evaluation and Excavation at Nos 36-58 Brownlow Hill 1997 and 1998. NML (unpublished).
Philpott R.A. 'Romano-British Merseyside since 1986' *JMAS* **12** (forthcoming).
Picton J.A. 1873 *Memorials of Liverpool 1 Historical 2 Topographical*. London.
Picton J.A. 1875 *Memorials of Liverpool, Historical and Topographical, 2nd ed.* London. Longmans, Green & Co. **1**. 156, 557.
Picton J.A. 1883 *City of Liverpool Selections from the Municipal archives and records from the 13th to the 17th century inclusive*. Liverpool.
Picton J.A. 1886 *City of Liverpool Municipal archives and records from 1700 to1835*. Liverpool.
Port Cities Liverpool (Mersey Gateway) website: :www.mersey-gateway.org/

Quartermaine J. 2007 Liverpool's Old Dock and the Maritime Trade of the North West. Oxford Archaeology website www.oau-oxford.com/html_ pages/maritime_trade.htm

Radcliffe R.D. 1890 'Schedule of Deeds and Documents [Crosse Family] Part 1', *THSLC* **41** n.s. **5**, 209-226.
Radcliffe R D. 1892 'Schedule of Deeds and Documents [Crosse Family] Part 2', *THSLC* **42** n.s.**6**, 209-226.
Radcliffe R.D. 1893 'Schedule of Deeds and Documents [Crosse Family] Part 3', *THSLC* **43, 44** n.s. **7, 8**, 330-352.
Radcliffe R.D. 1894 'Schedule of Deeds and Documents [Crosse Family] Part 4', *THSLC* **45 n.s. 9**, 221-234. Index to Crosse Deeds Parts 1-4, 235-240.
Richardson J. 2003 *The Local Historian's Encyclopaedia* 3rd ed.
Ritchie-Noakes N. 1984 *Liverpool's Historic Waterfront, The Worlds First Mercantile Dock System*. London. Her Majesty's Stationery Office. 19, 21-22, 23, 27-28.
Rideout E.H. 1928 'The Old Custom House, Liverpool', *THSLC* **79**, 3-73.
Royden M.W. 1991 *Pioneers and Perseverance 1791-1991*. Countywise Ltd.

Sharples J. 2004 *Liverpool* Pevsner Architectural Guide..
Shaw G.T. and Shaw I. 1907 (1987 reprint) *Liverpool's First Directory* A Reprint of the Names and Addresses from Gore's Directory for 1766.
Smith H.E. 1870 'Archaeology in the Mersey District 1869', *THSLC* **22** n.s. **10**, 267-294.
Stewart-Brown R. 1910 'The Tower of Liverpool', *THSLC* **61** n.s. **25**, 41-82.
Stewart-Brown R. 1912 'Moore of Bankhall', *THSLC* **63** n.s. **27**, 92-119.
Stewart-Brown R. 1917 'The Townfield of Liverpool 1207-1807', *THSLC* **68** n.s. **32**, 24-72.
Stewart-Brown R. 1925 *Birkenhead Priory and the Mersey Ferry*. Liverpool.
Stewart-Brown R. 1932 'The Pool of Liverpool', *THSLC* **82**, 88-135.
Stonehouse J. 1852 'Historical notes, respecting the Township and Village of Everton', *THSLC* **4**, 66-78.
Stonehouse J. 1869 *The Streets of Liverpool* (facs).
Stonor R. 1957 *Liverpool's Hidden Story. Billinge near Wigan*.

Taylor H. 1902 'The Ancient Crosses of Lancashire', *TLCAS* **19**, 136-238, Liverpool section 190-194.
Telford A. 2002 An Archaeological Watching Brief at the site of the former St Paul's Eye Hospital, Old Hall Street. (unpublished).
Telford A. 2002 An Archaeological Watching Brief at the site of the former St Paul's Eye Hospital, Old Hall Street. Phase 2 (unpublished).
Touzeau J. 1910 *The Rise and Progress of Liverpool from 1551 to 1835* **I** and **III**. Liverpool.
Troughton T. 1810 *The History of Liverpool*. Extra-illustrated edition in Liv RO.
Twemlow J.A. (ed.) 1918 *Liverpool Town Books 1 1550-1571*. Liverpool and London.
Twemlow J.A. (ed.) 1935 *Liverpool Town Books 2 1571-1603*. Liverpool.
Tyrer F. (ed.) 1968 'The Great Diurnal of Nicholas Blundell of Little Crosby, Lancashire 1702-1711', *Rec Soc Lancs Ches* **110**.
Tyrer F. (ed.) 1970 'The Great Diurnal of Nicholas Blundell of Little Crosby, Lancashire 1712-1719', *Rec Soc Lancs Ches* **112.**
Tyrer F. (ed.) 1972 'The Great Diurnal of Nicholas Blundell of Little Crosby, Lancashire 1720-1728', *Rec Soc Lancs Ches* **114.**

Visitors Guide to Liverpool 1886. SMR reference.

Wardle 1946 SMR reference

Young H.S and Young H.E. 1913 in Muir R. 'Historical Description'*Bygone Liverpool Illustrated by Ninety-Seven Plates Reproduced from Original Paintings Drawings Manuscripts and Prints with Historical Descriptions by Henry S. and Harold E. Young'*.